CHARLES A. FERRIER S.

I loved to wander in the green lanes and woods.   Page 2.

THE STRUGGLES

OF

A VILLAGE LAD.

"THERE IS NOTHING LIKE TRYING."

––––––––

LONDON:
WILLIAM TWEEDIE, 337, STRAND.

LONDON :
RICHARD BARRETT, PRINTER,
MARK LANE.

CONTENTS.

THE STRUGGLES

OF

A VILLAGE LAD.

CHAPTER I.

EARLY RECOLLECTIONS.

AMONG the earliest recollections of my life is living
in a beautiful little cottage, in one of the pleasantest
villages in England.

It was situated at the bottom of a green lane, and
before it ran a clear stream of water, which was always
rushing and gushing over its pebbly bottom. In front
of our house was the garden, which with the cow and
pig occupied all my father's leisure time. The poultry,
which consisted of ducks and geese, were under the
control of my mother, assisted by myself, Susan, John,
and Moses. Then there were the bees, which were
under nobody's control, so they did and went just what
and where they pleased. At the back of the cottage
was a small building erected by my father, assisted by
myself, in which our rabbits were kept, of which we
children were the sole proprietors, and as a matter of
course took great interest in. A brood of young rabbits
at that period of our lives was an affair of as much
importance as the birth of a young princess is to the
world in general.

In summer when our garden was in full bloom it was
worth walking a mile to see.

My father was what is usually termed, in village
language, a " handy man ;" that is he could do almost
anything he wished with a very few tools and scanty
materials. No employment pleased him more than to
beautify his cottage, and well was his labour repaid.

B

Before the door he had built a rustic porch, in which he had trained a honeysuckle, which during the time it was in full bloom gave a sweet perfume to all around. Then there was the grape vine, which was nailed to the wall, and went nearly the whole way round the house. It was a beautiful sight when the vine was laden with its purple grapes, its green leaves, the bright windows and the clean white blinds showing in contrast. In autumn the grapes were gathered and sent to market, and never failed to fetch a good sum of money, which my careful mother expended in such comforts as she deemed necessary for the winter.

In this retreat were spent some of the happiest years of my life. I knew no cares but such childish whims as crossed the path of every wayward child. Young as I then was, I loved to wander in the green lanes and woods, gathering wild flowers in spring, as I knew the names and properties of most which grew in our neighbourhood. Often, lying on some sunny bank, listening to the gurgling brook as it rushed at my feet, or admiring the flowers and leaves, wondering who made them so beautiful, and who made the winds to blow and the sun to shine, and why it was not always sunshine and calm.

These little trips into the woods were usually stolen ones, as I was forbidden to go out of the lane, for fear of being lost. To make amends for these trespasses, a large handful of wild flowers were usually gathered as a peace offering to my mother. Autumn was the time when most temptations were offered. There were the dewberries, as large as cherries, so sweet and delicious to our childish palate; and then there were the hazel nuts. Who could resist such tempting delicacies? I was not old enough to climb to the top of the hazels in search of nuts; so usually contented myself with picking up such as had fallen. This was the time to try our mother's patience with regard to our wardrobes; thorns would hang, and childhood was too impatient to unloose them, and therefore a short snatch was the readiest way to get rid of any hindrances, sometimes tearing the trowsers, the jacket, and in some cases the skin. If by some lucky bough we were enabled to get up the hazel shrub, in coming down, fearful of falling, we clung with our legs close to the tree, it was not unlikely an unfortunate prong of some kind would catch our trowsers, and tear the leg from the bottom to the top. Such an accident usually caused some little uneasiness in our minds as to what mother would say to us when we got home.

Well do I remember the strong warnings that were usually given before we went out in the morning. It was as follows :—" Now, Frank, I hope you do not mean to go into the wood to-day ; for if you do you will be sure to get lost."

" Yes, mother."

" No, you mean, Frank."

" Yes, mother."

" Now, mark my words, if you go into the woods, getting nuts and tearing your clothes, I will punish you when you get home."

A mother's threats are something like thunder, awful to hear, but seldom dangerous. So it was with my mother : she had promised this punishment so often that we began to think it all a fiction, and almost wondered what it really was after all. The usual punishment, if such it could be called, was, " Now, sir, unlace your shoes, and go to bed directly." This we were nothing loth to do, as we were tired, and usually fell asleep immediately. On awakening, confessing our crime, and promising not to do the like again, we were released, and, if possible, happier than ever.

In this manner passed the first eight years of my life, without anything occurring worth recording, when an accident happened which put an end to all my wanderings. One day I had been told to go on some errand to the village ; but in my carelessness I forgot what it was all about ; and, it being a beautiful warm day, I rambled off into the woods, where I remained till nearly dark. In vain did my mother search and enquire for me everywhere. Alfred Day, a boy who usually went with me, said he had seen me in the morning standing by Ball's-pond. Surely I had not fallen in and was at the bottom. Just as the neighbours had begun to assemble with clothes-props, manure-hooks, and the like, to search the pond, Billy Goon, an idiot, said he had seen me go down Valley Lane about one o'clock. This created a new diversion, and I must have gone to the woods and got lost. Just as they were on the point of starting off with lanterns, to look for me, I was descried by some juveniles coming up the lane with a great nosegay of wild flowers, which I need not say failed to make my peace this time. No sooner had I arrived at home than a consultation was held, and the result was that the next week I was to be sent to school.

CHAPTER II.

MRS. CORNER'S CLOCK.

IN our village there was no lack of schools. There was the Grammar School, where none were allowed to go but gentlemen's sons; then there was the National School, taught by Mr. Pepper, who used to cane the boys and girls so much that they all declared it was a shame. Besides these, there was the dame school, the mistress of which did not cane the children, but pulled their ears, and pinned them to her apron. The great question was, to which of these schools was I to go. Mr. Pepper, it was said, beat the children a great deal, and taught them but little; while Mrs. Corner did not beat them enough, but taught them a great deal. The Grammar School was out of the question; the National School was too far from our house; so it was decreed that I should go to the dame school.

This school was the terror of all little boys, and brave indeed must have been that boy or girl who durst have laughed in the presence of Mrs. Corner.

I see the school now, with its gable end next the street, with one window with diamond panes, in which always stood two flower-pots, and a jug with a broken handle holding some musk or golden moss. In front of the house was a garden, by the cultivation of which, with the assistance of her school, Mrs. Corner gained a livelihood. Leading up to the door was a paved walk, on which a spot of dirt was never allowed to rest. Then there were the monthly roses on each side of the door, and the grape-vine running just above it, out of the reach of any furtive fingers which might be tempted to pick them. Then there were the two windows in front, the white blinds, green shutters and door; and within that door sat the awful Mrs. Corner, near the window, always either knitting or mending stockings. In front of her was a small round three-legged table, on which lay her work, and to which we were called to say our lessons. Then there was the fire-place, with the fender and fire-irons so clean and bright that it made our eyes blink to look at them. On the mantelpiece were some china ornaments of a shepherd and his dog, a small tin tea-caddy, and another box which we could never understand. Above the mantelpiece were two pictures, and between them a string of birds' eggs. The most wonderful of all was a Dutch clock, which had a great picture of a basket of roses on the top. I never look upon a clock of that kind, even now, but I always think of that clock. I will tell you what makes me remember it so well presently.

The first lesson that Mrs. Corner usually taught was, how to scrape our shoes and wipe them on the mat, and then to make a bow on entering. We then took our seats on some low forms, and were taught the most difficult of all lessons to learn—the art of sitting still. When we had all assembled, Mrs. Corner made us kneel, put our hands up, close our eyes, and say a short prayer. When this was over, our lessons used to be recited, and woe be to that unfortunate who did not know the stipulated number of spellings! Mrs. Corner was a woman who said but little; but it was the way in which she used to look at us that frightened us. Not that she ever looked angry; but there was something at the corners of her mouth and eyes that said as loud as words to the lazy ones—Do you stir from this table if you dare! Mrs. Corner never told us that we spelled a word wrong; but as soon as a mistake was made she used quietly to take up her work, and with her peculiar look chain the unhappy little victim to the spot. Perhaps to get himself out of his difficulty he would commence spelling the unfortunate word again. Suppose it was righteousness, which was an awfully hard word: ri-ti, riti—ous, us, ritius—nest, ritiusnest. Mrs. Corner, on hearing her favourite test of learning thus grossly mis-spelt, would just smile and give her head a little toss, which never failed to set the little urchin crying with all his might.

Mrs. Corner was a woman who liked to have things done well, and, hard as we used to think her, yet we acquired an amount of accuracy in what we did which did not fail to have an effect on our characters in after life.

But about Mrs. Corner's clock?—yes, that clock formed one of the great events of my young days, and had an influence upon my character during the rest of my life. After I had been to school about a year, I began to be looked up to as a sort of authority in matters relating to Mrs. Corner's school, and took little liberties which none of the others dare think about, much less attempt. It so happened one forenoon that I was seated behind the mistress, and, to make the others laugh, I slyly stole a stocking from the table, and proceeded with great gravity to imitate Mrs. Corner, throwing out my arm just when she did, and dropping the corners of my mouth at the same time. At last she found me out, in a way that I little expected. In front of Mrs. Corner was a small looking-glass, and although I could not see her, yet she saw me.

When I had kept on till I was tired, she said, very calmly, " Are you tired, Frank?"

" No, marm."

" I thought you were," was the calm reply, " as you stopped imitating me."

I sat down, blushed to the crown of my head, and even now, although many years have passed away, I feel as though it were done but yesterday.

" Do you like to be idle, Frank ?" she asked, without looking at me.

I had always a great veneration for the truth, so I said, " Yes, marm."

" Well, you shall be as idle as you please this afternoon, and then you will see if it is as pleasant as it seems."

The afternoon came, and Mrs. Corner seated me on a stool in front of the clock, and told me I might fold my arms and look at the clock the whole afternoon. How pleased I was ; and that afternoon was grammar afternoon and I should have none to learn. How pretty the clock looked with its painted face, and the hands, and the weights, and the pendulum,—all of which I might look at and examine as long as I pleased. The first five minutes passed away very pleasantly ; but by the time I had looked at it for a quarter of an hour, I thought the pendulum moved much slower, and the minute-hand did not seem to move in the least. I tried to count a thousand ; but by the time I had counted fifty I began to think about something else, and my eyes to wander from the clock to other objects in the room ; but no sooner were my eyes off the clock than Mrs. Corner's rod was about my ears. Another quarter of an hour dragged slowly away, when I begged Mrs. Corner would let me do something, as I was tired of doing nothing. The only reply was a clip of the hands with the rod for not keeping my eyes on the clock. Another quarter dragged away, when Mrs. Corner asked me in her mild way, if it was not a pleasant thing to be idle. I begged and prayed for something to do ; but no—it was so nice to be idle. By the time I had looked at the clock about an hour, I grew desperate, and after stamping and crying for some time, all to no purpose, I caught up the stool upon which I had been sitting, and dashed it with all my might at Mrs. Corner's clock. Thus ended my school days at Mrs. Corner's; for after that she would have no more to do with me, as I was a dangerous boy, and might next time throw the stool at her.

That hour of looking at the clock cured me of idleness; for from that day to this I always feel the greatest horror of it; and though Mrs. Corner now lies in the old churchyard, my young friends may, in a great measure, thank her for this, and many other of my works. I never see an idle person lounging lazily about but I say to myself, you ought to go to Mrs. Corner's school for a short time.

Idleness my mother used to say was the gate through which all other faults usually crept. It is a thing which ought to be shunned above all things. Somebody has said its webs at first are like those of a cobweb: a child may break them; but, if unchecked, it grows with our growth, till it binds round us as tightly as the ivy to the oak, till at last the person has no power to help himself.

Shun idleness, my young friends, as you would a monster that would drag you into the worst misery. If you give way to it, you will never rise or make any great progress in the world. "Whatsoever thy hand findeth to do, do it with thy might."

Look around you, and I have no doubt but you may find plenty of instances where idleness has been indulged in during childhood, and at manhood has brought woe and desolation. Look at that poor ragged wretch just coming out of yonder ale-house! Ask him what first made him take to drink, and he will tell you not the love of the drink, but the love of the company. In other words, he first sought the ale-house to pass away an idle hour. And so with thousands of others, who but for idleness and drink might have stood foremost in the land. If you wish to be happy, respected, and a blessing to your day and generation, shun the vice of idleness. When you feel it coming upon you, think of Mrs. Corner's clock. "But I cannot help it," sometimes

I fancy I hear a little boy saying. Let me tell you, young friend, when such is the case, throw off your jacket, and turn up your shirt-sleeves, and if that does not frighten idleness away I do not know what will, unless it is a plan adopted in the East. If a person was idle, and no means could be found to make him work, he was chained in a cistern, in which the water was allowed to flow, and his business was to pump it out; if he was too idle to do it, the water soon gained upon him, and he was drowned. Thus, to save his life, he was compelled to make a vigorous effort, which is the only way to dispel idleness, as it is only the result of slow circulation of the blood. A vigorous use of the limbs is the best way to get rid of it.

CHAPTER III.

OUR SCHOOL.

It is a remarkable fact that, thirty years ago, when schools began to be first talked about, and it was found that a school must be had, a building was usually selected that could not possibly find a tenant. In large towns, a house that could not be let, on account of smokey chimneys, or some other inconvenience, was usually selected for a school; first, because it was cheap, and secondly, because no other tenant could be found. In country villages, where it was a difficult matter to find a house large enough to meet the wants of the village, some other building was usually selected, such as an old patched-up hovel that was useless for agricultural purposes. It was strange that farmers should feel more interested in the comfort of their cattle than their children; but such was the case.

It is often amusing to trace the history of a school,— how it struggled into existence, and managed, in spite of all opposition, to live and become a useful institution. The early history of our school is involved in some obscurity : some say that there had been money left by somebody who was crazy, and that a somebody not making his will very clear, and the people who were executors, not understanding their duties, allowed another somebody to get the money, and so the school was lost. The fact of having a school in the village had been looked upon as a fact, and an old garret over the church porch was fitted up for the reception of children ; but when it was found that out of a hundred a-year, which was to have been the endowment, only six pounds ten shillings and sixpence could be obtained ; the school was then commenced as a private speculation, and carried on in that manner for many years.

One morning the whole village was thrown into a state of excitement, by the fact that a young gentleman of considerable property had committed suicide. No sooner was that excitement over than another of overwhelming magnitude was spread, not only over our village, but all the villages within five miles. On reading the will it was discovered that the aforesaid young gentleman had left one hundred pounds a year to the parish of Melvale, and all the surrounding villages within the distance of five miles, upon condition that a suitable building should be provided by the inhabitants of Melvale. It also went on to say that all children should be admitted at one penny per week, of whatsoever religion, sect or denomination.

Melvale had, since the days of the Puritans, enjoyed one continual quarrel, the ground of which was the Dissenters hated the Church, and the Church-going people hated the Dissenters ; and so far was that dislike carried, that, in some instances, they would not marry into each other's families. The Dissenters looked upon the Churchmen as wicked wretches, and only fit for the company of a certain gentleman and his angels, and the Churchmen looked upon the Dissenters as long-faced hypocrites.

Now this one hundred pounds was a fresh bone of contention. The Church-people declaring that they had as much right to send their children to school as the

Dissenters, and the Dissenters as loudly proclaiming that they had equal privileges ; but, to a man, they declared that they would not contribute one farthing towards the building, unless the Church-people signed a paper to certify that they would not send their children to school, as they could not think of having the morals of their children contaminated by associating with the children of the Church-people.

Thus the struggle went on for several years. At last a gentleman who had an old barn, for which he had no use, offered to give them the free use of it, and fit it up for them with such things as were necessary for carrying on the school. No one opposed it, or assented ; and the school, or barn, was prepared, and a master and mistress appointed. A day was announced for the opening ; work was entirely suspended, and all hastened to see who would send their children, as the Church-people said that if the Dissenters sent theirs, they would not allow theirs to go ; and the Dissenters declared as emphatically that theirs should not enter the building if the Church-people sent theirs.*

The day came, but none would allow their children to enter : thus they stood cavilling, when the attention of the idlers was aroused by a troop of strange children, with a clergyman at their head, who with some difficulty made way for them to enter the school. Another troop, from some other village, made its appearance, another and another, and as the church clock struck nine, the school door was shut and locked. This both church and dissent declared it to be an insult, and that their children had as much right to be admitted as strangers. Then followed a knocking at the door, but they were too late. The master opened a door, which had been used for the purpose of pitching sheaves through,

---

* Some of my readers may smile at this phase of village life ; but is it more ridiculous than the great question of National Education, when every person says that they will have no National Education unless their peculiar views of religion are taught? While the cavil is going on we are losing the advantages, just as the good people of Melvale did the advantages of their school.

and held a parley with them. The result was, the school was as full as it would conveniently hold, and there was at present no room for them; but he had no doubt that when some of the children left,—in a year or two perhaps,—he should be able to accommodate them.

Thus commenced our school, and about five years after the above circumstances I was admitted into the awful presence of Mr. Pepper, the master, who declared I was one of the finest boys for my age that he ever saw, and he was sure, and proud to say it—that he should make a fine scholar of me in a short time. This would have sounded pleasantly enough, I have no doubt, had not Mr. Pepper told every father and mother the same tale since the school had been opened. What a contrast are our modern village schools to that one. I have the old school before me, just as it was on the day I entered. The building was about 144 feet long by about 40 broad, with an open triangular roof. The floor was of clay, which was always cold and damp, and was, without doubt, the cause of many an untimely death by sowing the seeds of consumption. The walls were of various material, some places boarded, and at others lath and plaster; but as the wall was only one thickness, it was no difficult matter to run a stick through it if we wanted to peep through into an inn yard at the back, or hold a little private conversation with any of our friends who might chance to be there.

With regard to ventilation, not even the most fastidious of her Majesty's Inspectors of Schools could find the slightest fault; for what with the holes in the door, the broken windows, and the cracks in the walls, the winds could sport in and out as they pleased.

In summer this ventilation was agreeable enough; but in winter we suffered most dreadfully. Scarcely a boy could be found but had chilled feet, and it was no uncommon thing to see a dozen boys huddled round the school stove with a real or sham ague. This last was not at all unfrequent, as it usually gave them a seat by the fire till the fit was over, which was prolonged as long as convenient.

The usual allowance of coals to warm the school during the winter was thirty bushels; so that for the last three months there was no fire.

Such was our school at the period when I entered; yet with all this misery in the winter season I have seen as many as 200 children in it. The mystery was how they managed to learn anything, as Mr. Pepper seldom taught; it was as much as he could do to keep order among so many.

———

CHAPTER IV.

A TRIUMPH.

It was a custom in our school once a month to give the boys test sums to work out, to ascertain if they understood the rules which they had been learning. The boy who had worked them best was promoted to the top of the class, and so with the rest in proportion to their merits. If a boy could maintain his position at the head of a class twice he was then promoted. It was the highest ambition of every boy in the school to get there, as he had certain rights and duties to attend to which gave him authority, and there is nothing that boys, or men either, like so much as authority.

Now I had set my mind on being first at the next examination. The rule which I was then working was compound subtraction, which proved to be very difficult to me. I could not understand how I could get sixpence from fivepence, and that would leave elevenpence. Alfred Day and Tom Slack saw it clear enough; but I could not understand the process of borrowing a shilling when there was no one to borrow it of.

I have often heard father say, "If you cannot do a thing at first, think about it." I did try to think; but as soon as I began to think about my sums something else would be sure to come into my mind. At last I said, as all idle boys and girls usually say, "I don't care. I am sure I shall never be able to understand it, because it is so hard." Not harder for me than Alice Slack or Alfred Day : they can understand it, then why cannot I ? "Because you have never really tried, Frank," was the answer of a still small voice within; "or you would be as well able to do it as they are."

I had often heard father say a person may do almost anything they chose, if they really try, and try in good earnest. I will try to-day, I will listen to the explanation, and I will understand it, if possible. "Alfred," said I, " set me a hard sum on my slate, and I will see if I can do it this noon." I well remember how I ran down the lane leading to our house, and crept through a hedge, and sat down on a green bank and began to reckon. I saw it ! I did it ! and there it was in good large figures.

What is the use, as father says, for any one to wish for a thing if they never try for it ? There is nothing like trying ! after all, if we do but try in real earnest !

When any one has done a good action, or achieved some point which they had been striving for a long period, what a feeling of importance it gives us ; how we are apt to envy those below us who have not been so fortunate !

With what authority I walked into the school, and with what pity I looked down upon those who could not understand the rule. There I was, looking with certainty to be the head boy in the class ; but a still small voice would whisper, " You are not there yet Frank."

The day came at last, and, with my slate fresh washed, and my pencil newly pointed, I felt myself quite equal to the task. At half-past ten Mr. Pepper came to the class, and gave us each a small paper, on which were written four sums,—these were expected to be done in half-an-hour : if they were not done in that time it was supposed that they could not be done at all. My sums are done, and I have no doubt they were right. Alfred Day had done his, and so had Tom Slack and Alice.

The slates were examined in silence. Mr. Pepper never said whether they were right or wrong, and no one could tell by his looks. At eleven o'clock the list was written out just as we stood. One boy was promoted to the upper class, and Frank West stood first; then Alfred Day, Tom Slack, and then followed the rest according to their merits.

With what dignity I moved about the school—the head boy in the class, with all the responsibility of going to seek all absent ones, carry messages for the master to the parents, prepare all the wants of the class, report to the master all late comers, and assist the monitors whenever I was wanted. What a giddy height it was for a boy to obtain: but those who are high have many winds to shake them, and so it was with me. I soon found that a good thrashing was no uncommon thing to those holding the office of assistant monitor, from boys whom I had caused to be punished; and that was not the worst of it. They frightened me almost out of my senses, by saying they would tell Mr. Pepper that I had been using bad words, and that I set a bad example. Though I was perfectly innocent, yet I knew if such a report was told to the master I should be degraded into a lower place, and perhaps severely punished. Thus was I made miserable in the office which I had striven so hard to obtain.

I have often heard father say that the greater part of our pleasures arise from imagination. We see an object in the distance,—it looks beautiful,—we try to obtain it, and when that is accomplished we soon see that it is not all we expected. At the distance we only see the tinsel and ornaments; but, on closer inspection, the object which we have been at such pains to obtain is full of what we most dislike. So it was with my situation as assistant monitor. I had expected to have had absolute control over the children, and often blamed others for not having; but they held control over me in a manner that I least expected. So it is in the world: we blame others for not doing as they ought, little imagining the secret spring that prevents them from doing their duties.

CHAPTER V.

A GREAT UNDERTAKING.

When I had been in the school about two years and had worked about as far in arithmetic as the boys usually went in our school. Few boys ever went beyond the Rule of Three. When that was finished Mr. Pepper sent them to the beginning of Reduction again, and it was whispered among the boys that even Mr. Pepper could not do the practice sums, they were so hard. How it was, I do not know; but I conceived the idea that I could go through the book. I knew I could,—somebody must have done the sums at some time or another, and why could not I? "Try, Frank," I said; "but have you counted the cost before you make up your mind. It is easy enough to make good resolutions; but not one in a thousand can put those resolutions into practice."

These thoughts were running through my mind one cold evening in autumn as I was on my way home. How welcome home looked, with its glimmering light shining through the window. It was the centre of my world, the place where I could turn when all else was dark and frowning. And what was that one thing which rendered it so attractive? *Love for each other.* If one was in difficulties, we all felt for him or her; and if any little triumph was achieved we were all equally delighted. It was a love of home when I first went into the world that preserved me, with the assistance of God's grace. If I commit such a sin, what will father, mother, John, Susan or Moses say? were usually my thoughts.

I am afraid my young friends will think me a talkative old man, and that I ought to go on with my story. Well, well; all I can say is this: I only wish to bring before you that which held me in the straight and narrow path, so that you may have the same guide as I had.

When I arrived at home John and Susan were busy assisting mother in preparing the evening meal against father returned. I went out, split the wood, fed the rabbits and pig, watered the cow, and did all there was to do, except milk, which father always did.

"What a deal of work a boy may do if he will only give his mind to it," said I, as I washed my hands and face; and besides I ought to do it. Only think what a while father has been at work in the fields, and how tired he must be when he comes home!

How cheerful people always feel when they are busy and have their hearts in their work. So it was with me. I felt very happy as I took up little Moses from the floor where he had fallen after a vain attempt to pull my slate from the table on him.

At the usual hour my father's well-known step was heard coming up the pathway leading to the cottage. This was the signal for all to be in action; Susan to set his chair and arrange the cushions, John to open the door, and mother and I to place the supper on the table. Then arose a sharp competition as to who should unbutton his gaiters and unlace his boots. This was usually ended by taking Moses on his knee, and resigning one leg to Susan and the other to John.

When supper was over, and Moses sent into banishment for the night, I took down the old slate, and washed it thoroughly, thinking at the same time a good beginning made a good ending, as I had often heard father say :—

"Now point your pencil, and you are ready for work, Frank West."

With what alacrity did I turn over the leaves of my old tattered arithmetic, and with what perseverance did I work that night, and one sum after another was done, till I came to the last, and that was a hard one through which I could not see. Do what I would to it, it came out wrong, and how vexing it was when I had filled my slate with figures, and felt sure it was right, and on looking at the answer it was a thousand pounds out of the way. I figured and then rubbed them out, till at last I got careless, and finally declared I could not do it. Then I began to play with the cat and tangle my mother's sewing cotton, and in fact do anything but what I ought to have done. Then I began to talk to father about school, and how clever I was, and how I knew almost as much as Mr. Pepper; and that if I lived I had made up my mind to work through the arithmetic.

" But, Frank, have you counted the cost?" said my father. " Do you know the difficulties you will have to overcome? You ought to think well before you make up your mind."

" I have, father, and I am going to do it."

" But you will never do it," said he, " by talking about it. To accomplish anything that is of any great worth you must work—ah, and work hard, too!"

" See here, father, I have done all these to-night," said I, looking like some one who had done a wonderful action; but at the same time I felt I had not done all I ought or might have done.

" But why not finish this rule to-night and start fairly on another to-morrow evening?"

At this I hung down my head, and murmured, " It was so hard, and I could not do just that last one."

" My son," said my father, giving me one of his peculiar looks, " I am sorry to find you, like the greater part of the world, making resolutions you have not the power to put into practice."

" But it is so hard, father."

" That is just it. If all the sums had been as easy as those you have done you would have gone on well enough I have no doubt. Thus when your work was easy, and no difficulties in the way, you went on very well; but at the first difficult sum you say you cannot do it. Tens of thousands have done exactly what you have done to-night—started well in the highway of life, full of good resolutions, determined to persevere; but, like my son, at the very first difficulty to be encountered have stopped, and all the persuasion in the world could not get them to give another fair and honest trial."

" But father," said I, " will you help me."

" Frank," said he, " I would willingly help you, but

I would much rather you would strive to help yourself. A boy, or man either, who cannot do that is but badly prepared for the world. Such persons generally live by the labour of others, and are therefore an hindrance to society. Yes, my son, learn in your young days to look upon difficulties as things of everyday occurrence; strive to overcome them, and the strength you will gain in overcoming one difficulty will help you to overcome the next. Life has been compared to a journey, in which there are hills and vallies. What would you think of a person travelling, who, at the first hill he came to instead of mounting the hill one step at a time, went round it rather than over it? You would say he was hindering himself on the way. So it is with many people. While one man is looking at and fretting over his difficulties, another overcomes them; and thus some men thrive so well in the world, and others cannot get forward in the least."

" But, father, don't you think this sum is a very hard one?"

" Not so difficult but it can be easily done if you go to work the right way. The fact is, you have made up your mind that you cannot do it, and consequently you have not the resolution to give it another fair trial."

" But do you think I could do it if I tried?"

" Yes, I think if you were to give it one fair and honest trial you would be able to do it in a few minutes."

" I will try," said I, and to work I went again. I read the sum over and over again. I saw it. " There! I have done it," said I, thumping the table with my fist; " I am sure there is nothing like trying; is there, father?"

" No, my son; and for want of that one last vigorous try many a good and deep-laid scheme has failed."

CHAPTER VI.

OUR SCHOOL LIBRARY.

In our school was a small library of about twenty books. How they came to belong to the school, no one seemed to know. Mr. Pepper said he found them in a drawer when he took possession of the school, and he had occasionally lent them to the children as a reward for their good behaviour. I had long looked forward to the distinguished honour of having a library book to read at home. How I came to like reading I am unable to say; but I often think it was through listening to the tales of my mother, of which she always had such a plentiful supply. Whatever she heard or read she remembered, and then produced it in her own words. In this way I learned a great deal of my scripture knowledge. Before I was twelve years of age I could have given nearly the whole of the histories of the principal characters mentioned in the Old Testament. The life of our Saviour was also a very favourite topic, and to which I listened with the greatest zest, and thought my mother one of the most wonderful women.

" Mother," said I, one evening as I skipped into the house, " what do you think?"

" I do not know, Frank. Why?"

" I am so pleased!" and then I snapped my thumbs and fingers so violently at little Moses that I made him cry. Then I had to take him off the floor and hug him till he was good. " There," said I, setting him down on the floor, which was his own dominion, and giving him my slate to play with.

" I wish, mother, you would guess what has happened; but you cannot: so I must tell you."

" Yes; do, Frank," said Susan.

" It is a secret, Miss Susan, and I shall not tell unless I like."

" But I know what it is. It is about Ned Hicks' donkey."

" No, it is not."

" What then ? Now you will tell me, won't you, Frank?" said Susan, coaxingly.

" Well, then, Mr. Pepper said if I behaved well till Friday I should have a library book."

" I am pleased to hear it, Frank," said my mother: " it shows that Mr. Pepper has a good opinion of you."

The long-looked-for Friday came at last, and I was allowed to choose a book—the first book that I had ever read. How I turned them over to find the best ; my choice being fixed upon that one which had the greatest number of pictures in it. I well remember that book. It was entitled " Keeper in Search of his Master." To me in those days this was a most wonderful book : I read it through, and then began it again, and as firmly believed it to be the truth as I believed my own existence. Then when " Keeper in Search of his Master" was returned, there was that book of all books, the " Pilgrim's Progress," with some of the most wonderful pictures I had ever seen. With what rapture did I dwell upon poor Christian running from the City of Destruction, and plunging into the Slough of Despond ! And then there was the hill on fire ready to tumble down upon his head. Then how delighted I was when good Mr. Evangelist, came and set him in the right road, and pointed to him the wicket gate through which poor troubled Christian was to get into the strait and narrow way that leads to life eternal. All this I believed to be literally true, and in after years it was with difficulty I was brought to believe that it was not so. I loved this book : its simple style, its novelty and freshness, gave me a love for reading, and, best of all, it gave me visions of future bliss which will only be forgotten when I cease to live, and I trust may be more fully realized when that awful day shall come. When poor Christian's troubles had been cried over, till I had seen him safely ferried over the dark river, and enter the Celestial city, the book was returned. The next book was Robinson Crusoe. How delighted we all were over this book, and believed every fact we read as readily as

if there had not been such a thing as fiction in the world :
and for anything which we knew there was not; for we
had never heard of people making books which were not
true.   How sorry we were when it was finished! But
John declared he would go to sea, and get shipwrecked
as Robinson Crusoe did; for he thought it must be a
mighty pleasant life to live all alone on an island in the
wide ocean, and then find great lumps of gold, and come
home again by some means, and write a book about it.
Susan said if she were a boy she would be a sailor, and
go all over the world, and come back rich and happy.

Thus we read book after book till we had read the
whole library, and then we read them again.   Not only
did I read the books, but I strove to remember what I
read ; and I have no doubt had I been asked I could
have told not only what they were about, but have given
nearly the contents of the whole of them.

I have often heard father say, that reading without
remembering what we have read or gathering instruction
is no better than idleness.   " There are three sorts of
readers," he used to say: "those who read for instruction,
those who read for amusement and instruction, and
those who read in idleness.   I hope my children will
not resemble the last."

The school library—and it is a great pity there is not
one attached to every school—gave me a taste for reading
which has since been an endless source of instruction
and amusement.

It was a custom of my father's, after we had read a
book, to examine us, to see if we remembered what we
had read, or fully entered into the meaning of it.   In
this way reading was a source of amusement, and at the
same time we were filling our minds with ideas which
were of use to us through life.

I often think what an important thing is the first
book a parent or teacher puts into a child's hands.   I
believe it often tells upon the child's future life.   If the
book is amusing and interesting so that he can understand it and knows what he is reading about, (as a little
boy once told me,) he will wish for another, and another

book, till the habit of reading is formed, and then, like all other habits formed in childhood, it is difficult to break. On the other hand, a book is presented to a boy : let us suppose he is expected to read it,—he does read it ; but it is probable by the time he has got to the end of it that he does not even know what it is about. No curiosity has been excited, and there is no wish to read another; consequently that boy looks upon reading as a dull affair. How different would it have been if the book had been written in a style he could understand. With what interest he would have followed the thread of the story. How, with beaming face and lighted eye, he would have sympathised with the character in the story. One book read and well understood, and the child thirsts for another, and a source of amusement has been opened to that child's mind which will often keep him out of folly and sin. You have opened a door by which he may obtain knowledge which may fit him for this life and the life which is to come. I do not wish to tire my young friends with my prosy remarks, and have them lay down the book and call me a stupid old man ; but bear with me, it is for your good that I write it.

But to my story. All the books in our school library had been read ; and now you will think I was satisfied. No; for by it a thirst for reading had been created which I am thankful to say has not been quenched to this day, and I trust will not as long as life lasts. How to satisfy my thirst for reading was a question that neither myself nor John could answer. We knew father could not afford to purchase books ; but the proverb says, " Where there is a will there is a way ;" and the way in which I accomplished it must be the subject of the next chapter.

CHAPTER VII.

I AM MADE A MEMBER OF THE PEOPLE'S LIBRARY.

I HAVE often heard father say when a person really wishes for a thing it is surprising what efforts they will make to obtain that object; and so it was with me. How to get books—that was the question. Susan said she had been with mother to the next market-town, and she had seen lots of books,—a cartload she thought, and all to be sold.

"Yes, Susan; but the money—the money," said I. "Where is that to come from?"

It appears that Susan had not given that a thought.

John suggested—"Would it not be nice to have a library of our own?"

"Capital!" said I.

"As big as Mr. Pepper's?" For John had once seen that great library, which, if reports are true, was nearly as large as the clergyman's.

"Yes, John; but the money,—only think how much it would cost!"

"I wish we could earn some by some means."

Now this had never struck me before. "Yes," said I musingly, "earn some,—yes; but how, and where? That is the point. What could I do? And even if I could get work, father would much rather that I should go to school. If it was harvest, I could get plenty to do; or getting potatoes; but that is past long since. If I were a girl, like Susan, I could knit stockings and sell them; but that is girl's work."

While I was thus pondering, who should come up but George Lightley. "Frank," he began, "have you heard the news?"

"No," said I; "what is the matter?"

"Charley Beal, the postman, has got his leg run over, and the doctor says it is hurt very badly, so that he will not be able to get out for some time to come."

A thought struck me that I might do his work for him during the time he was ill; so I asked who was going to manage the post-office for him, as I knew Mrs. Beal could not, for she could neither read nor write.

"I heard," said George, "that Alfred Day was going to ask for the place."

"That is just the place for me," said I, musing. "I am sure I can do all Charley used to do. I am sure I can make up the letter-bag; I have seen him do it many times. And then I can carry round the letters, and be in time for school." Here I laughed a good round laugh at the idea of being postman, and away I ran to see Charley. "I am sure he will let me do it," said I; "for I have done it for him many times when he has been poorly. Why I am just the one to do it."

On my arrival at the post-office I was much disappointed when I heard that the doctor had given orders that he was to see no one, but was to be kept perfectly quiet.

"I only wanted to ask if he wanted any one to attend the post-office now he is ill."

"I wish, Frank, I had known that you would have done it for us," said Mrs. Beal—"you would have been just the boy; but I have promised it to Alfred Day not an hour since."

"It does not signify, Mrs. Beal," said I, turning away to hide the great big tears that were starting in my eyes.

"Never mind," said I; "what is the use? I dare say there is something else to do in the village besides carrying letters. I do wish I had known it sooner: but I went as soon as I heard of it; so I cannot blame myself for not attending to it. I don't care," said I, at least twenty times on my way home; but it is a certain fact, that when a person says they do not care, they have the most cause to care. When I had reasoned myself into a calmer state of mind, I began to see, after all, it was not so bad. "Why, now I think of it, that is just the place for Alfred Day; for I know his mother is very poor, and I had rather Alfred Day had got it than any other boy." Thus ended my first attempt to earn money.

For days I was on the watch, but nothing turned up by which I could earn anything. "I wish father was rich," said I one day as I was going home, "and could buy all we want; or that fairy days would come again, and some good fairy would come to our house, and turn all the old things into new ones. I wish she would come. What a sight of things I would give her! There is the bellows that I have so much trouble with every morning when lighting the fire. Then there is Susan's Sunday bonnet, and my book, and the old hatchet—fairies! why everybody knows there are no such things. But I do wish—wish!—but what is the use of wishing? I have often heard my father say wishing without working is like ploughing without sowing. If I were like George Lightley I should not care. He goes to school when he likes, stops at home when he pleases, and has just what he likes, he has only to ask his mother. While I am obliged to go to school, like it or not; and as for having anything that I want—I never think of asking, because I know father and mother cannot afford it, and it makes them look so uncomfortable.

One day a number of boys were lying on the green in front of the school when a cart-load of coals went down the hill into the village, and a discussion arose as to the merits of the team. George Lightley said his father's horses were the best in the village; Alfred Day and Will Greaves said that Farmer Ball's horses were the best, and if they were sold would fetch double the money of George Lightley's. In such-like talk we were engaged when the cart stopped and shot down the coals in front of Dr. Brown's door. As quick as thought I ran down the hill, and by the time I reached the Doctor's the perspiration was running down my face. "If you please, sir," I began, but was unable to proceed. "If you please, sir," I began again——

"Well, well," said the Doctor, who was very deaf, and, like most deaf people, he thought everybody else deaf. "Now what is the matter—any one killed?"

" If you please, sir, I want to get the coals into the cellar for you."

" The what—the colt in the river? What did you let it get there for? I can do nothing for you. Stop: tell your master as soon as he gets him up to the farm I will come and bleed him if it is——"

" There is no colt in the river. The coals, sir."

" Who has got a cold?"

" Please, sir, I want to shovel the coals into the cellar for you."

" I suppose I must give you a draught of some kind, and a few pills. Come this way."

" No, sir," I shouted again; " I want to get the coals in the cellar." At the same time I caught up a shovel, and pointed to the heap.

" The coals, to be sure; I did not understand you. What is your name? I ought to know your face."

" Frank West, if you please."

" I thought you went to school, Frank. I heard your father say so."

" Yes, sir; but I want to earn some money to buy a book, and I can do that and go to school as well."

" Of course you can," said the Doctor. " Now let me see how nicely you can do this little job, and then we will see about you."

I got the barrow, threw off my jacket, turned up my shirt-sleeves, and to work I went; but I soon found it was not so easy as I expected. " Never mind," said I; " a little at a time, and one may work wonders." In two hours the coals were all in the cellar, and nicely packed in, the road and path swept, and the shovel and barrow put carefully away. With what pleasure did I look upon that heap of coal so nicely packed up, and all done a little at a time.

" Now I wonder how much he will give me?" were my thoughts as I rang the back-door bell. " It cannot be less than fourpence, and perhaps sixpence. I never had a silver sixpence in my life."

" So you have done your work, Frank?"

" Yes, sir."

" Well, what am I to give you?"

" What you please, sir."

" So you want to buy books, do you?"

" Yes, sir."

" And how much money have you got towards them?"

" I have not any yet. This is the first I have earned."

" I cannot understand what you want with books."

" If you please, sir, I want to read them."

" Are you fond of reading?"

" Yes; only I cannot get books to read."

" I see," said the doctor, musingly—" one of the great faults of our system of schools. We teach children to read, and then give them nothing to read; and what is the result?—when they have left school three or four years they forget nearly all they have learned."

I did not know whether the doctor was talking to me or to himself; so I replied when he stopped, " Yes, sir."

" Of course it is so. I will tell you how you can get the use of a thousand books for a shilling, and even more than that, if you choose."

I thought that Dr. Brown was taking leave of his senses.

" I like you, Frank, and I will give you this shilling, or I will pay one quarter's subscription for you in the People's Library at Welton. Now which shall it be, the library or the shilling?"

" The library, sir, if you please."

" I am going to Welton this afternoon, and, now I think of it, I can let you have three books now. One is on Insects, another on British Birds, and the other on the evils of Drunkenness. You can take them now," said the good old man, seeing my impatience to grasp the precious treasures. " There, run away now, as I am busy, and when you want any more come to me."

" Father is right, after all, when he says everything is ordered for the best. Now, if I had gone to the post-office I should not have belonged to a library. I belong to a library!" (and here I drew myself up to my full height at the important fact), "and all through my own exertions. A thousand books!" said I, wondering what they could all be about. I had no idea there were so many books in the world.

I have often heard father say that we cannot get anything that is worth having without trying, ah! and good vigorous trying, too. Some people go creeping through the world, grumbling as they go, because times are bad; but I often think if they were to give a good vigorous try to better themselves there are few but could do it.

CHAPTER VIII.

A NEW IDEA.

No sooner was I fairly out of the doctor's gate than home I ran as fast as I could with my books, and bursting into the house, nearly upsetting my mother who was cleaning the floor. "Mother," said I, "see here!" at the same time holding up the books. "Do you know how I got them? No, I am sure you don't; I will tell you. Doctor Brown lent me them for getting his coals into the cellar, and he says he will get me as many as I like to read for three months."

"Oh, do come and look!" said Susan, throwing down the scrubbing-brush with which she was helping mother. "Do come and look at these pictures. The book is full of them. Won't you let me read this one, Frank? I am sure it is a nice one, because it has got so many pictures in it."

"Yes, you may read it; and when John comes home he may read this; only the doctor says that you are not to tear them, nor turn down the leaves."

About half a mile from our house was a wood, through which was a path seldom used except in the hunting season.   Across this path lay a tree which had been blown down.   To this place I repaired with one of my books; it did not matter which, as each was equally interesting to a mind thirsting for knowledge.

The book that I had brought was upon the " Evils of Drunkenness."   Here in this calm retreat, with nothing but nature around me, I first read of the evils of drunkenness.   That summer afternoon will never be effaced from my mind.   All nature was calm and serene; no sounds were to be heard but the gentle sighing of the wind, the chirp of the birds, and the hum of in- sects, and now and then the cawing of a rook; these rather lulled my mind than disturbed it.   I read till it grew dark, when I turned my steps homeward, think- ing the whole way upon what I had read.

As soon as I could get an opportunity I began to question my father upon what I had read.   " Father," I began, " this book says that drunkenness is the curse of our nation."

" Well, my son, and what of that ?"

" If it is, why do people get drunk ? "

" Because they like the sensation or feeling which intoxicating drinks produce."

" If it is a curse to the country why does not some- body stop it ? "

" Why it is not done, is simply because people don't seem to know how to stop it.   The question is how is it to be done ?   If you can solve that question, I have no doubt that it would soon be done."

" Why, it is easy enough, father."

" Easy, my son ?" said he, " resting on his spade."

" Why yes.   Now look here; if every person under twenty years of age, were to say that they would not touch any more strong drinks, in forty years, or less, there would not be a drunkard in the country."

" You are right, my son.   But now comes the ques- tion.   How are you going to persuade all the young people to abstain from strong drinks ?   If you could do that, your plan would answer well; but while the people believe that strong drinks are necessary for their welfare, whatever you may think or wish, they will not give it up."

"I don't know," said I, for I could say no more; "but I cannot think how it is that people become drunkards, as I cannot bear the taste of beer."

"And God, in his infinite wisdom, grant that you never may! But to your question—how people become drunkards. It is done as all other things are done,—a little at a time. No man becomes a drunkard all at once, but by little and little. I once heard a man say, who was a notorious drunkard, that when he was a young man he had no relish for strong drinks. 'My first step,' said he, 'towards becoming a drunkard, was through going to a public-house on a Sunday evening with some young men, instead of going to chapel. I knew it was wrong, and in my own mind resolved not to go again; but how frail are all our resolutions! I went again and again, till it became a regular habit. By degrees, I did not confine myself to Sunday evenings, but I went also on week-day evenings. Pleasure parties were proposed, time lost, an increasing desire for drink grew upon me; but after all, it took ten years to make me a confirmed drunkard.'"

"I will never become a drunkard," said I.

"That man, when he was as young as you, thought the same, and he fell; and I see no reason that you should not become a drunkard, unless you resolve never to touch it. If you have sufficient resolution to put that into practice, by the blessing of God, you are safe."

"Are there many people living without intoxicating drink?"*

"Not so many as there might be, for it is my opinion that people could do much better without it than with it."

"Tell me how it is a curse to the country; for I cannot see how drunkenness can affect the interests of a nation. I thought at most it only affected those who got drunk."

* At the time of which I am writing, the Temperance question was scarcely known.

"It is calculated that there are sixty million pounds sterling spent every year in intoxicating drinks. Think of the frightful amount of misery which must follow the expenditure of such an immense sum of money. But the expenditure of it is not half the evil; look at the crime which it produces. If you were to calculate all the charges which come before our magistrates, I believe that ninety-nine out of every hundred are the result of drink in some way or another. Now, to punish these cases, whole armies of policemen must be kept, prisons must be built and supported, judges must be paid, and a thousand other things which I cannot think of. Then look at the dreadful amount of poverty it produces, and the result is that hundreds of thousands of pounds more have to be paid in the shape of poor-rates. Now you may wish to know who has to pay for all these things. The industrious. I believe, if sixty millions are spent upon drink every year, much more is lost in repairing the evils which the drink has caused. If you wish to know what drink has done, go to the prison, and ask the first prisoner you see what was the cause of his being there, and he will answer—the love of drink,—lost character,—no employment,—theft followed, and here he is! Go and ask the man that is now a captive in the hulk, and you will hear the same tale. Go into our unions and lunatic asylums, and you too frequently hear the same story. Go into a hospital, and you will find that three-fourths of the accidents are the results of drink. Ask that poor trembling mechanic, whose feeble hands can scarce hold the tools by which he gains his bread,—ask him what brought him to that state, and if he deals fairly with himself, he will say it is drink. • Ask that poor grey-haired old man, who is often seen wending his way from door to door, how he became so wretched and destitute, and he will tell you, if he speaks the truth, that it was drink."

"But, father, you surely do not mean to say that all misfortunes are caused through drink?"

"No, certainly not; but if we could trace the greater part of these misfortunes which we daily see around us, we should find that very many of them, either directly or indirectly, had their first origin in drink. I often think, on viewing the matter calmly, that strong drink seems to be the agent sent by God to punish mankind; for wherever we find a nation given to intoxicating drinks on a large scale, either sooner or later that nation is doomed. If we look back into the history of the world, we shall find that those nations which indulged in intoxicating drinks, soon began to degenerate in the manly virtues, and soon became physically enfeebled, and were finally overpowered by a more hardy and vigorous race. Not only may we look at the histories of empires, nations, and kingdoms, but in persons generally; for wherever a love of intoxicating drinks prevails sooner or later it leads to evil."

I had never heard my father speak so eloquently before on any subject; but what he said sank deeply into my mind, as no doubt it was intended.

"I will never be a drunkard," said I, "nor will I ever laugh at them any more; for they are more deserving of pity than laughter. If we see a man who has lost his senses how we pity him; and is not a drunkard the same? All the difference that I can see, is, that the drunkard does it voluntarily, and the other does not."

CHAPTER IX.

THE ORIGIN OF THE BAND OF HOPE.

FOR weeks and months I reasoned and thought upon what father had said, and what I had read. What a dreadful thing it would be if I should become a drunkard! or John, or Susan, or Moses; and father says we may, unless we never touch strong drinks. Now I will make up my mind never to drink any more, and I shall be safe; but then there is Susan, John, and Moses,—I should not like them to become drunkards. Suppose I persuade them to do the same. "Now that is capital!" said I, flinging up my cap for joy, which the wind blew

D

into the branches of a tree. Here my agreeable re-flections were cut short by having to climb the tree to get my cap. There! " it is down into the pond," said I, beginning to descend the tree. These disasters put an end to my good intentions for that time; but, as father often says, if the seed is put into the ground properly, a crop of some kind is sure to follow : and so with my good intentions on never drinking strong drinks.

A few days after the above circumstances had occurred, we were all gathered together on the evening of a wet day. On fine evenings we were all busy at work in the garden. Father was reading ; mother was mending my jacket ; Susan was knitting, and John was dividing his time about equally in learning the multiplication table and teaching puss to jump over his hands. It was his intention, he said, when she could jump well to teach her to leap through a hoop, the same as the tigers do in the wild beast shows. I was working at the *Tutor's Assistant*, into which I had waded over head and ears into the most overwhelming difficulties.

My father at length took off his spectacles and laid down the book which he had been reading.

Now is the time to bring my subject forward thought I. Yes,—but I do not like; it does seem so strange. Make up your mind and do it, father would have said, if he had known I had been wavering. " Father," said I, at last.

" Well, Frank," was the mild reply.

" I have been thinking."

" I am glad to hear it, and if your thoughts were of any worth, perhaps you will tell us what they were about ?"

" I was thinking that I should not like to be a drunkard."

"God forbid that you ever may, or anyone belonging tome !" said my father, fervently.

" You said the only way to be safe would be never to touch it."

" I did say so, and that is my firm opinion."

" Then, father," said I, standing up and giving the

table a mighty thump with my fist. "From this hour I will never touch another drop of strong drink, and then I shall rest in peace that I shall be safe from being a drunkard."

"Amen!" said my father, "God in his infinite wisdom keep you, as he kept Joseph of old, in this wise and virtuous resolution. I wish that all my children would do the same."

"Do you really, father?" said Susan.

"Yes, my daughter; for in doing that you will shun the gate through which hosts of temptations flow."

"Then I will say, as Frank has said, that I will not touch another drop of strong drink."

"No more won't I," said John, throwing down the cat and his multiplication tables together.

"Father, a thought has just come into my mind."

"What is it Frank?"

"Why, that we form ourselves into a society; each one trying to get another to join us."

"That is a very wise thought, my son."

"What name shall we call our new society?" said I, half-wild with joy at the success of my scheme.

"Now I have something to propose," said my father; "and that is, all who join our society shall vow not only to avoid strong drinks, but that they shall attend a place of public worship at least once every Sunday, and oftener, if possible, unless illness prevent."

"But the name, father—the name of the new society; we must have a name."

"You must give it a name, Frank, as you were the founder of it."

John suggested "The Drink Reformers."

Susan said she thought "The Drunkard's Friend" would be better.

Mother thought "The Good Samaritans" would be a good name.

"I have it!" said I, "as all sober people are hopeful people, I propose that we call it "The Band of Hope."

"Yes, that will do nicely, said Susan. "Don't you think so, John?"

" Capitally !"

And the Band of Hope we called ourselves. Susan got pen, ink, and paper, and I wrote in a good round hand :

" We, the undersigned, do vow from this time forth never to drink any strong drinks, and to attend a place of public worship at least once every Sunday, and as much oftener as possible."

[Then followed the signatures.]

" FRANK WEST, sen.
" FRANK WEST, jun.
" JOHN WEST.
" SUSAN WEST, sen.
" SUSAN WEST, jun."

" How about Moses, mother ! He must be one."

" Of course !" said my father. " Fetch Moses, Susan."

" But he cannot write," suggested John.

" Then one of us will write for him : and besides, when he gets older I am sure he will be thankful for what we have done for him."

" Yes, that I am sure he will," said mother ; " and I will be answerable that he makes a good member of the society."

" Here he comes," said I. " Now Moses, my angel, take the pen. Not so ; there, that is the way. Bless his dear heart, how good he is, and how he stares ! I should not wonder but he has some idea what he is about. You take hold of his hand, Susan. There, now he has made a great blot. Never mind, I can scratch that out to-morrow. There, that is the way. Moses West. × Now I vote we give him a kiss all round, and send him to bed again ; for he begins to look most precious wide awake, and you all know when he is awake there is no peace." Then Moses was kissed all round, and sent again into banishment.

" Now, my children," said my father, when we were again seated, " we will, like the saints of old, when the Lord had shown them a favour, praise him for his past and present mercies." Then taking the great Bible— the Bible which had been his father's,—he read the touching story of the Prodigal Son, and then concluded with an earnest and feeling prayer, asking that God would look down upon our humble efforts in striving as far as lay in our power to do his will on earth. He then prayed that the little seed which we had that night sown might be watered with heavenly dew, and, like the mustard-seed, might in his own good time spread over the whole earth.

When the prayer was over, he addressed us, as near as I can remember, in the following words :—

" My dear children, what we have done to-night, I feel assured, will in time work much good, if you are determined to carry out your intentions. Remember, as I have often told you, that things will always grow if properly attended, but it must grow of its own natural strength. If we attempt to force a plant, it will thrive amazingly for a time; but when the forcing ceases, the plant withers and often dies. So it is with hundreds of societies which spring up : the promoters are so sure of their success, that every effort is made and every means adopted to raise money that can be thought of. The society thrives amazingly to outward appearance; but when the excitement has passed away, or the forcing of the plant, the members drop off one after another till only a few of the faithful supporters are left. These few get disheartened, and the society gradually comes to an untimely end. In my time I have seen the best of intentions ruined in this manner,—societies which would have been a blessing to thousands if the intentions of its promoters had been properly carried out. If you wish your little society to thrive, do all you can to persuade others to join you; but if you attempt to excite— which I do not think there is any fear of your doing— I have generally known those persons who enter any society in a state of excitement will be the first to leave it when the excitement is over."

After this came the evening prayer and the " goodnight kiss," as we called it; we then retired to our humble beds and enjoyed a sleep that kings might have envied.

CHAPTER X.

DOCTOR BROWN AND THE BAND OF HOPE.

" Susan," said I, " who do you mean to try to get to join the Band of Hope ?"

" I know, Frank ; but I shall not tell, unless you tell me who you intend to get."

" I mean to try to get Alice Slack ; she is such a funny little thing. I do all her hard sums for her, and she is going to make me a marble bag as soon as she can get a piece of strong stuff to make it with."

" Now is it not curious that you should fix on Alice while I have fixed on her brother Tom. I like Tom," said Susan, blushing at her thoughtlessness ; " he is such a good boy ; he always spells my hard words for me, and one day he carried me over the brook when the bridge was broken, because I should not get my feet wet ; just as if wetting one's feet would hurt any one."

" Why, Susan, sure you did not let Tom Slack carry you over the water ?"

" But I did."

" I would not have let him carry me over."

" But I did, just to see if he could carry me, and to see how I liked it."

" But it is not proper for girls to be carried on boys' backs," said I, gravely. " Suppose he had dropped you in the water."

" I should not have cared a bit, because I have waded through it scores of times, and shall again, I dare say. I like it," said she, catching up her school-bag and skipping-rope, and running down the garden-path, singing,

" I'd be a butterfly."

" I wonder what I shall say to Alice about the Band of Hope. I know it is of no use to say anything in the play-ground, as she will not have time to listen if I do. If I talk during school-time I shall get punished. Yet I do not like to say anything to her, because she laughs at me so, and calls me a funny little man ; but I am as tall as her brother Tom, and taller. Never mind," said I, at last, " I can but try ; " and with these comforting words I began to prepare for school.

" Frank," said Susan, as I entered the play-ground, " I have seen Tom Slack." Here Susan commenced skipping.

" What did he say," said I, eagerly ?

" Just what I expected."

" What was it ? Do tell me, Susan, all about it."

" There, that makes me just seven hundred."

" Did Tom say so ? "

" Why, no, you silly boy ! I mean that makes me seven hundred skips, and I intend to do a thousand before I go to school."

" Now do leave off skipping for a minute and tell me what Tom said."

" Well, he says he does not mind joining if there is plenty of fun in it."

" That is just like Tom," said I, in a tone of disappointment.

" Don't be angry, Frank, I know Tom will join us, it is only his fun you know. Have you asked Alice ? "

" No, I have not seen her."

" She is in the school, I saw her go in a few minutes ago."

In a short time the silence of the school-room was broken by one of the loudest and merriest laughs I ever heard. As soon as Alice could speak, she began with, " Well, I never ! What a funny old man you are, Frank, do tell me all about your wonderful scheme again, it is so curious."

" I cannot, Alice, you laugh at me so much," and at the same time the tears started in my eyes.

" Never mind, Frank ; I did not mean anything you know : but I could not help laughing, it did seem so queer, and you looked so serious. But do tell me all about it again, and I won't laugh if I can help it."

Then I told her all about the Band of Hope,—how all who joined it vowed never again to drink strong drinks, and always to go to a place of public worship at least once on a Sunday, and as much oftener as possible; and concluded with—" Now Alice, won't you join us."

" Yes Frank, I will join you if you have plenty of tea-parties, and lots of fun after."

" But won't you without, Alice? Now do; and then I will do all your hard sums, spell all your hard words, and lend you my knife to sharpen your pencil whenever you want it."

Here Alice went off into another long laugh, but finally came to reason, and said, " Well, I will be one of you, Frank."

" Thank you, Alice. But you know you are to try to get another to join us."

" I am sure I can do that. Our Jane will join I am sure : so will mother ; for I have often heard her say she wished there was not such a thing on the face of the earth as strong drink."

At the close of that day our new society had gone up to ten. We had all got a new member except mother and Moses. Susan had got Tom Slack, I had persuaded Alice, John had persuaded Alfred Day, and father had persuaded James Johnson, who was a sensible labourer that worked with him.

As I lay upon my little bed that night, I could scarcely sleep for joy, at the prospect of our new society thriving so rapidly. I also resolved the next day to try at a far higher prize, which was no less a person than Doctor Brown. Good old Doctor Brown! He has gone to his last resting-place long since; but his memory is cherished by all who knew him.

He was one of a race long passed away. With us boys he was a great favourite, and there was not one among us, but would have gone any distance with medicine for him on the darkest night, if it was not through the churchyard, or up Deadman's-lane. He was a very tall, broad-shouldered man, with a great bony hand, which, when laid upon any of our heads, nearly covered it all over. He appeared to be a man, who, by vigorous exercise in his youth, had laid the foundation for a life of health.

He usually wore a large broad-brimmed hat, from which flowed upon his shoulders long tresses of grey hair. Round his neck he wore an old-fashioned silk handkerchief, tied in a knot, with the ends tucked in the bosom of his shirt; grey coat, red plush waistcoat buttoned up to his chin, corded knee-breeches, blue worsted stockings, low shoes, fastened with large silver buckles, a walking cane in his hand, and you see him as I have seen him thousands of times.

I have often noticed, as I have gone through life, that children as if by instinct will follow some people who are perfect strangers to them, and talk and chat, as freely as they would to their own parents; while another person whom they see every day cannot get a word from them. I do not pretend to explain how this is; but such is a fact; and Doctor Brown was one of the former. Children would love him, and do anything for him. If he wanted a boy to go a couple of miles, one was always to be found; but if Mrs. Breezy, who was the Doctor's housekeeper, wanted one to sweep the back yard, or run on an errand, not a child of any sort was to be found.

Doctor Brown was never married, but for all that his house was always full of children. As soon as one batch was sent away, another swarm was sure to arrive.

Not only was he the healer of all the diseases which the human flesh is heir to, but he was the umpire in all disputes. If a person was in want of advice, the first person to whom he would naturally turn was Doctor Brown. If a disagreement occurred in the village, he was the mediator. The usual termination to all disputes was "Well, we will hear what Doctor Brown says." And most unpopular would that person have become, who would not have abided by his decision.

Not only had he brought nearly all the parish into the world, but he had also helped many of them out again. I do not mean to say that the doctor made bad work in his profession; but people must die, and when Doctor Brown could not save them, he helped them out of the world as easily as possible.

Not only did he practise the healing art, but he was

the executor of nearly every person's will. He also carried in his breast the secrets of nearly the whole parish. All difficulties and disappointments were referred to him, and usually terminated in—" What would you have us do, Doctor ?"

If any inquisitive person wished to pry into his affairs, or their neighbours, through him, he would patiently hear what they had to say, and if he was obliged to reply, his usual answer was, " A still tongue makes a wise head;" or, " The least said soonest mended, neighbour;" and then turn the conversation to something else.

As I before said, I had made up my mind to speak to the Doctor about the Band of Hope, and, if possible, get him to join it ; because I well knew that if he recommended it to the people, they would at once believe it an excellent thing.

Full of this idea, I resolved upon going that day during the dinner hour. The only excuse I had for calling upon him was to change one of my books. As the time approached, I wished I had not made up my mind so readily. It is an easier thing to make resolutions than it is to carry them out, as father says ; but, as I have made up my mind I must do it. I have heard father say, he would not give a straw for a man, or boy either, who makes resolutions, and then cannot put them into practice. With all my reasoning, my heart beat as I raised the knocker of the back door.

" Well, my boy, and what do you want ?" said the sharp voice of Mrs. Breezy, who disliked children as much as the Doctor liked them.

" If you please Mrs. Breezy, is Doctor Brown at home ?"

" Do you know who you are talking to, eh ?"

" Yes, marm."

" Ah! now you talk. Tell me what you want in five words ; for if I stand talking here, I shall get the rheumatics from head to foot ; I did not get a wink of sleep all last night with the pains in my head and face, and all the stuff the Doctor has in his shop will not cure them. Dear me! dear me! nobody knows what I suffer;

and so I may: I am sure no one cares for me. Now do tell me what you want."

" If you please marm, I called to see if the Doctor was at home, and if so, can I see him."

" Is that all? for I don't want to be running back-ward and forward three or four times."

" Yes, marm." ·

" You have not got any of those nasty, stinging beetles about you, I hope!"

" No marm, I am sure I have not."

" What is your name?"

" Frank West, if you please."

Now, I ought to have observed that the Doctor, among his other pursuits, was very fond of Natural History, and had given all the boys in the parish com-missions to bring him anything they could lay hold of which appeared curious, all of which Mrs. Breezy called stinging beetles, and of which she seemed to have the utmost horror.

In a few minutes I was ushered into the Doctor's private room, where I found him busily engaged in examining some curious moths which had that morning been brought to him.

" Then you have come to see me again, Frank?"

" I suppose you want your books changed?"

· " If you please, sir, I want one of them changed. I have not finished the others yet."

" Keep them as long as you please."

" I think this book will suit you," said he, taking a volume from the bookcase. " It is on the Wonders of Nature."

" Thank you, sir: I am sure I shall like it. "Seeing me hesitate, he asked me if all were well at home.

" Yes, sir." It never occurred to me till then the difficulty I should find in making the Doctor understand me, as I before stated that he was remarkably deaf. At length I began with " Please, sir, I want to speak to you."

" What did you say? You must speak out, or I can-not hear you."

" I want you to join the Band of Hope."

" Give you a piece of soap?" said he, doubtfully.

" No, sir!" I roared at the top of my voice. " Don't you think strong drinks are hurtful?"

" Tom Dicks hurt himself, eh?"

" No!" I shouted again.

" I cannot make out what you are saying, child," said he, going to a drawer, and taking out an ear-trumpet. " Speak in this end," said he, applying the other to his ear.

" I am come to ask your advice about the Band of Hope."

" The Band of Hope! And what may that be child?"

I then explained to him all our plans and views, and finally asked him if he did not think strong drinks were hurtful?

" Of course they are. I could have told you that forty years ago. It never struck me before; but you are certainly right. Upon my word, Frank, I did not think you had been clever enough to have invented such a scheme. What a stupid old man I must have been, not to have thought of some such plan long ago, to stop the evils of drunkenness! Why, it is just the thing for every one! It is the way to keep them in health, and in wealth too. Besides, if it does no other good, it will give those who abstain from drink a good moral character, and that is not to be despised in these days. Yes, you are right, Frank; and I will join you with all my heart, and do all I can to bring forward your views in the village. For the present, I wish you good day, as I am busy just now."

" Hurrah!" said I, throwing myself down on the grass as soon as I was fairly out of sight. " I have done it now! I trust in a few years that drunkenness will only be known by name, and talked of as a thing of the past. There is nothing like trying, as father says. I might have wished a long time before anything would have been done. Act, that is the point, and act now: now is ours, to-morrow may not be. Father always says when a thing has to be done, do it."

CHAPTER XI.

MY FIRST EMPLOYMENT.

I HAD now arrived at the age of eleven years, and it was deemed a great shame that I had not been sent to work above a year ago. "What is the use of so much learning to a boy who is to follow the plough all his life? It is all very well for them," said Farmer Ball, "to be able to read their Bibles and Prayer-books, and to know as much arithmetic as will enable them to reckon up their week's wages; and, as for writing, why I see no use in it. A fuss is often made about poor people being able to write their own letters. I say it is all nonsense: they have no letters to write; and, besides, if a servant-girl can write, she can read writing. And what is the consequence if you leave your letters about? Why the whole world will know your business. No, no," said Farmer Ball, with a wise shake of the head! " education and emigration is the botheration of this country." And then the old gentleman used to laugh and chuckle as if he had said the most clever thing that was ever thought of.

Not only was this Farmer Ball's opinion, but of hundreds of others, and is at the present day. The parents gladly fall into the same opinion, as it releases them from the burden of paying for their children's schooling, and at the same time adds a few pence to the family income.

How little do parents imagine the harm they are doing their children by taking them from school at such an early age! Who can tell what is buried in the mind of a child, which might, with culture, wake up the genius of a Milton, a Shakespere, a Watt, or a Stephenson? A word spoken, sometimes when least expected, may turn the current of a child's mind, and awaken such thoughts as may with reflection cause him in after years to become one of the greatest benefactors to his species. But, alas! this is denied to the agricultural poor, as their employers think that they are only created to be machines for life.

It was the opinion of Farmer Ball that I was quite old enough to work in the fields, and I do not think my father dared to interfere, even if he had been so inclined; for in doing so he would most certainly be a "marked man," and would have lost his situation at the first slack of work : which in our village would have been a most serious matter ; for if one farmer discharged a man for any supposed fault, it would have been considered an insult to his former employer for any other farmer to have employed him.

Monday morning, at half-past five o'clock, I was aroused, and in a few minutes was at Mr. Ball's farm, wondering what I should have to do.

"So you have crawled here, have you, you young snake?" were the words with which Farmer Ball greeted me on my arrival. "You ought to have been in the fields an hour ago."

"If you please, sir, I did not know that you wanted me so early, or I would have been here."

"Now don't please sir me ; I am not used to it, and I do not want it. Now do you hear?"

"Yes, sir."

"You go to Noon's Folly field, and keep the crows, birds, and other vermin from my corn, and if you let so much as a lark rest upon it, I will thrash you beautifully. Now be off with you, and don't you go to sleep, or I will make you remember it."

I was glad to get out of the presence of Farmer Ball, as he always frightened me, and away I posted to Noon's Folly, which was full three miles from home, thus having six miles to walk morning and evening, besides walking about nearly all day.

I cannot tell how hard I worked that day ; but do all I could the birds would alight upon the corn,—when I frightened them away from one end of the field, they only appeared to fly to the other. In vain I ran shouting, and as loud as I could, but all to no purpose. It seemed that the birds did not understand me; but I think I must have annoyed them most unmercifully.

After running about till I was in a most profuse perspiration, and almost ready to drop with fatigue; for be it known, when a boy goes into the fields first, the change of temperature from heat to cold or from cold to heat, affects him most sensibly—even strong men are tired out in a few hours, when going from shelter to work in the open fields, when I was about throwing myself under the shade of an oak tree to rest, I heard a well-known voice calling to me. Where the voice came from I could not conceive. At last, who should make his way through the hedge but Alfred Day.

" I say, Frank, what are you making all that noise for? You will kill yourself. Who are you tenting for? " *

" Mr. Ball."

" He did not tell you to make all that noise, did he? "

" He said I was not to allow a lark to rest on the land; and, do what I will, I cannot keep them away."

" Well, I never! Why what a precious innocent you are! Do you suppose you can keep the larks away, and many of them got young ones too? "

" I do not know," said I, pitifully; " but I must try, I suppose. How do you know the larks have got young ones now? "

" Because I find them every day, and so could you if you pleased. I will show you how. Now look yonder. Do you see that lark, hovering with outspread wings over the corn. There, did you see her drop?"

" Yes."

" Run to the place, and you will find a nest of young ones; but don't meddle with them."

" What will Farmer Ball say if I do not frighten them away?"

" He knows very well that small birds do no harm, as they mostly live on seeds and insects."

* Bird attending or minding.

"What did he say I was to do it for when it cannot be done?"

"He said so to keep you awake. All you will have to do is to be here about four o'clock in the morning, as the crows usually feed about sunrise, and then perhaps they will come again in the middle of the day; but it is only in very dry weather that they take to corn."

"But why in dry weather, Alfred?"

"Crows usually live on worms, slugs, and insects, which they find in the ground; but when the earth is very dry the worms get into the earth so deep that the crows cannot reach them, and then they come to the corn."

"Then I shall have nothing to do but keep away the crows."

"The pigeons are the worst, as they come at all times of the day."

"I see," said I, "it is only to crows and pigeons that I shall have to 'tent.'"

"That is all."

"How thirsty I am, Alfred! Have you any drink with you?"

"Come with me; I will show you some beautiful water at the bottom of this field. It runs out of a land-drain into a hole I have dug for it; and it is as cold as ice. I do not know what I should have done without it. Here it is," said Alfred running down a steep bank into a water-drain. "Now tell me what you think of this," said he, as he came up the bank with his hat full of water. "Don't you call that the right stuff? Now I must go, as I see the crows are coming to see us."

"How do you know?"

"I will tell you. They never come in flocks the same as pigeons, but one or two at a time. There is one now, sitting on yonder gate. I have no doubt she is the first. You will see her drop into the corn directly, and another will take her place; and so they will keep coming one or two at a time till the field will be covered with them."

" But what does that crow sit on the gate for ? Why does she not go to the corn at once ?"

" There are always one or two watching, and if there were any number in the field the moment she saw you she would give a caw, and away they would fly, and out of sight in one minute."

" She has flown away ; she knows my old red waist-coat as well as you do. Now I must go back again, I will call for you when it is time to go home."

Thus I was taught the art and craft of " bird tenting."

How slowly the time seems to pass away when one has nothing to do, which I had not for four or five hours at a time. I wish I had brought a book with me, it would help to pass away the time. I wish there were some willows growing here, then I could make a whistle, or a windmill, or a puzzle of some kind.

Night came at last, and with it Alfred Day ; and my first day in the fields was ended. I wanted no reading that night, but sleep, which I soon found on retiring to bed. I thought I had but just laid down when I heard my father's voice calling me to rise : " Come, Frank, it is struck three, don't you hear Alfred Day calling you?" There was no help for it but to rise, and half asleep I dressed, found a book, and not forgetting provisions for the day, I walked briskly on by the side of Alfred Day ; and before the sun was up we were both at our respective fields.

I had never been in the fields so early before ; but even to me, accustomed as I was to country life, the scene of light and shade, the cobwebs which had been spun in the night, all glittering with dew ; the singing of the birds, and the thousand delightful objects, filled me with wonder. There were the various wildflowers, with their different odours and colours ; the gambols of a hare across the path, the cry of the partridge, the crow of the pheasant, the chirp of the quail, the singing of the lark, the bleating of the sheep, the barking of a distant sheep dog, the cawing of the rooks, the striking of the village church clocks, which on a still summer's morning may be heard for miles. All these to my young mind were objects of wonder and admiration, and young as I was, I could not behold these beauties of Nature without feeling something stirring in my breast like love to their Creator.

I continued my employment for several weeks without anything happening worthy of notice, when an incident occurred, which in the end materially altered the course of my life.

CHAPTER XII.

BRIGHT PROSPECTS.

I have often heard father say that there is no such thing as luck; but good or evil fortune is much the result of our own seeking. If a man is careless or indifferent with his worldly affairs, he is generally unlucky, if he leaves the gate of his clover field open through carelessness and his cattle get in and kill themselves with eating the clover, we say that man is very unlucky. If a man takes a business he does not understand, and does not succeed, he is unlucky. On the other hand, if a boy at school is careful to gain all the information he can, and stores it up in his mind, there are many chances in the world by which that boy may rise, and such are usually called lucky fellows. It was a common saying of my father's, as we sow in youth so we must reap in manhood, and if we fail to plant the mind with useful ideas none can grow, and instead of virtue will spring up vice.

In my career through the world, I have usually found my father's sayings pretty correct with regard to things in general. " If I see a man," he often said, " in an alehouse of a morning, I can generally tell that his business is neglected. If I find a man in bed half the day, I usually find that man unlucky. If I see a man gossipping away his time when he ought to be at his work, it is a sure sign that he will not have work to do long. If a man leaves his business for pleasure, his

business will leave him and bring sorrow in its place."
"As we sow so we must reap," are the words of Holy
Writ, and every day we may see those words fulfilled.

Time passed merrily on with my "bird tenting," for the
greater part of my leisure time was spent in reading such
books as Doctor Brown brought me from the Welton
library. I cannot say how it happened, but the Doctor
usually selected such books as suited me, but in truth
I was not particular. There were Tales, Stories, Maga-
zines, Travels, Poetry, Biography, History, Religious
Tracts, &c., all of which were read, and it seemed the
more I read the more the craving for books increased.

One day as I was lying under the shade of a tree, a
gentleman came from the road to ask me the way to
Welton. I was on my feet in a moment, and making one
of my best bows, I began, " If you please, sir, yonder
is the church," at the same time pointing with my finger.

" Yes, I see it; but which is the road, my little
fellow ?"

" You see this road, sir ?"

" Certainly."

" Then go straight along till it turns, and then you
will be at Bear's Cross ; then turn to your right for a
quarter of a mile, and then you will see a bush ; you
turn down by the bush into Brook Way; the next
turning is to the right, and the next to the left, and
you will come to the mill-stream. You must mind the
stepping-stones, as one of them is lose, and if you do
not mind how you tread, it turns over with you."

" How deep is the brook, if this unlucky stone should
turn over with me ?"

" Not more than up to your knees, I should think."

" Is there no other way to the town than that ?"

" Yes, sir, but it's three or four miles further
round."

" I think you are a keen little fellow."

" Thank you, sir."

" What book have you in your hand ?"

" If you please, sir, it is ' Simpson's Euclid.' "

" Can you understand it ?"

" Yes, sir, pretty well, thank you."

" How far have you read ?"

" I can do most of the first book, but I do not understand the second book."

" Are you fond of such books ?"

" Yes, sir, now I can understand them."

" Who teaches you ?"

" No one. I get a piece of chalk, and make the figures on the road or anywhere, and then I read the book, and if I cannot understand it, I think about it for a while, and I am sure to understand it at last; and so you see it is nice amusement."

The stranger paused, and after looking at me from my bare feet to the crown of my rough head, he pulled out a shilling, and said, " There, I will give you that if you will prove to me that two sides of a triangle are greater than the third side."

" Yes, sir, I can do it; and I will show you how to do as many as you wish. This is an easy one."

In a few seconds I had drawn the figure with my stick on the road, and in one minute I had gone through the proof.

" That is cleverly done," said the gentleman, " and here is the shilling."

" No, thank you, sir, I do not want it. Shall I show you how to do some more ?"

I saw the gentleman smile, at what I took to be my kindness.

" Why won't you take the shilling ?"

" Please, sir, I do not want it."

" Don't you want anything that a shilling will buy ? Cannot you remember anything you want ?"

" No, sir; I have plenty of books from Welton, and that is all I want at present, thank you."

" Are you fond of reading ?"

" Yes, sir."

" What books have you read ?"

" I have read—let me think. I have read ' Pilgrim's Progress,' ' Jack the Giant Killer,' ' Watts' Hymn Book,' and learned all the ' Divine Songs;' ' Keeper's

Travels,' ' The Song Book,' ' Watts' Logic,' ' Dick Turpin,' ' Æsop's Fables,' and——"

" A mixture, certainly ! but what did you make out of Watts' Logic ?"

" I could not make much out of it; but it amused me."

" You will be a great man some day," said he, smiling.

" I don't know, sir; mother says she thinks I do not grow any."

" I do not mean so ; I mean you will be a learned man."

" I had rather be a good man, like father." I always looked upon my father as the best of men, and even when grown to manhood I never had cause to change my mind.

" But," said the gentleman, " how would you like to be both good and learned."

" I should like it above all things."

" To what trade does your father intend putting you ?"

" I do not know; but Farmer Ball says that I am to drive plough after the harvest."

" Pity—pity," said he. " I suppose you have left school ?"

" I do not know; but when there is nothing to do in the fields, perhaps I shall go for a month or two."

" Can you do sums ?"

" Yes, sir, I have worked nearly through the ' Tutor's Assistant' without any help, and after harvest I shall finish it."

" Should you like to go to the Grammar School ?"

" Yes, sir; but father cannot afford to pay for me."

" Do you know me ?"

" No, sir."

" I hope we shall know each other better some day."

" Thank you, sir."

" I am the new master of the Grammar School."

" Indeed, sir !"

" In October next there are to be three boys admitted into the school free of cost, and if you like you can try to get one of the scholarships. There will be an examination, and those three boys who acquit themselves the best will be admitted."

"If you please, sir, on what subjects shall we be examined?"

"There will be questions from the Scriptures, Grammar, History, Arithmetic, and the First Book of Euclid."

"Can any boy try?"

"Yes, if they are of good character, and can bring a certificate of baptism, and a written recommendation from one of the trustees."

"Thank you, sir; I should like to try, if I knew when it was to be held."

"I will let you know when it is. What is your name?"

"Frank West."

"Frank West," said he, writing it down in a pocketbook. "Good day, Frank; I will remember you, and I have been much pleased with you."

Some of my young friends may say I was lucky in meeting with this gentleman; but was it luck that impelled me to work through that hard old arithmetic; was it by luck that I knew the First Book of Euclid. No, it was by working out one of my father's maxims: "Make up your mind to do a thing, and do it." "Fortune," he used to say, "always knocks once at every man's door, and it is well to be ready for her coming."

CHAPTER XIII.

DOUBTS AND DIFFICULTIES.

"October," said I, musingly, when the gentleman was gone, "and this is July—only two months. I wonder who else will try; perhaps Alfred Day. I wish he would, as it would be so nice to have him for a companion, as I do not know any of the other boys, and it will be lonely at first. I do not care for that. I have heard that to get into the Grammar School is as good as three hundred pounds; but I am sure I do not know how much that is, more than I ever saw. Then I shall have all my clothes and food found, and live in a beautiful house, and have nothing to do but to learn for three or four years. I hope father will let me go. I am sure he will. That will be better than driving plough for Farmer Ball."

If father had heard me talking thus he would have said, there is many a slip between the cup and the lip. "Nonsense," said I at last, "how foolish I am talking in this way, why I am talking just as if father could afford to pay fifty pounds a year, and I was sure of going, when there is nothing more unlikely; but I have heard father say, that half the world take shadows for realities, and that is why so many people meet with disappointments.

How slowly the hours passed away that day, I strove to read, but before I had read half a page my mind was wandering to the Grammar School; at last I laid the book down, and bounding over the hedge I went in search of Alfred Day, to whom I told my tale of the Grammar School. Someways the subject did not seem to interest him so much as I had expected, and when I had finished, he cooly remarked : " Is that all ?"

" Yes, but won't it be nice, Alfred, to get into such a school ?"

" Of course, but it is my opinion that you will not get there."

" Why, Alfred ?"

" There are at least ten reasons for it."

Now, I always had a great opinion of Alfred Day's ideas, on any subjects which came under the notice of us boys, he always saw things in a clear straightforward manner. If he said a kite would not fly, we knew it was next to useless to try it; if a boy bought a new top, and he said it was worthless, the peg would be out in a few days, not a boy in the school would give a marble for it. Thus Alfred became an authority on all matters of interest to the whole school.

"But why do you think I shall not be able to get into the Grammar School, Alfred, I resumed?"

"In the first place, I do not think you are scholar enough, and that is a very strong reason; and, another thing, I have no doubt that there will be a great many at the examination who have had better opportunities of learning than you have."

"But suppose I do know enough?"

"That is what every one thinks almost. George Lightley, who you know is the head boy in our school, thinks that there is not another boy knows so much as he does, simply because there is not another to contrast with him. I have heard somebody say, that we never know our ignorance till we by some accident get into educated society, and then we are ashamed of it."

"But, Alfred," said I, much disappointed at the light way in which he seemed to speak of my abilities, "Don't you think there may be a chance?"

"Yes, you may have a chance; but, at the same time, I would not give you three marbles for it."

"Well," said I, when I was by myself again, "I can but try, and the right and only way is to work hard at the subjects which the gentleman named."

"Come here, Frank," said a well-known voice as I was going home, "I have something to tell you, which I am sure will please you." The person who was speaking was George Lightley.

"I shall be glad to hear any news if it is good," said I.

"That is just like you, Frank, always talking so much about good and bad; why we cannot speak without fear of putting the words in the wrong place. I am not going to the National School any more, I am going to the Grammar School, and father is going to hire a private tutor to get me on, ready for the examination, which is to take place in October. I am glad I am going there, as mother says the National School is only fit for the children of the lower orders. Will it not be grand, Frank? They do not admit anyone there who are not the sons of gentlemen."

"I think, George, the examination is to be open to all classes who choose to try, and if father will give me leave I intend to try."

"You try! That is good. You may try, but I do not think they would admit such a boy as you, unless it was to clean the boots and shoes. I should like to see you go to the examination as you are now, they would think you were going to beg."

"I shall hear what father says when I get home, and it is not you, George, that will stand in the way."

"My father is one of the trustees, and he will see that you do not get there, and if you do not mind, I will teach you to speak a little more respectful to your superiors."

"Oh, George," I began.

"Don't George me; I am Master Lightley if you please, and I beg that you will think no more about the Grammar School, for I heard Mr. Ball say that he intended to make a plough driver of you after the harvest." Here he burst into a loud laugh.

I turned away to hide the tears that began to roll down my cheeks. "I did not think George would have spoken so unkindly to me," I murmured, when out of his hearing. "I who have worked his sums many times to save him from being punished, and now for him to triumph over me in this manner, it is too bad."

"Never mind," said I, "words are only wind with such a boy as George Lightley, and all the fretting in the world won't mend it. We shall see in October who is the best. I hope father will let me go, I will ask him to-night, as soon as I get home."

"Father," said I, as soon as I entered, "may I go to the Grammar School?"

"The Grammar School!" said he, "surely Frank you have lost your senses, or you would not ask such a question. What else could have put it into your mind?"

"But if there was nothing to pay, and I could get in, would you have any objection to my going?"

" Certainly not, but I am sure there is but little chance of your getting there free of cost; and as for being paid for is quite out of the question. I have given you the best education that lies in my power, and if you ever wish to rise in the world, it will have to be by your own exertion."

" But suppose a good fairy has been to me to-day, and told me something."

" There are no such things as fairies, Frank, and I do not wish my son to believe in such nonsense."

" If I could by any means get there would you have any objection?"

" It would be the happiest day of my life to see you so fortunate, but that can never be; a life of toil lies before you I fear, and you must make up your mind to bear it."

" You have surely not heard the news, father?"

" News, child! what are you talking about? you seem half wild about something."

" Yes," said Susan, " I have heard the news; potatoes are cheaper, and it is always so when we have any to sell; and onions are dearer, just when we want to buy."

" Now Susan, do hold your idle tongue, and let me talk if you please."

" Do you know, father, that there is a new master at the Grammar School?"

" Yes, I heard of it; but what of that?"

" He has been to me to-day, and offered me a shilling if I could work a problem in Euclid."

" Which of course you could not;" said my father.

" Yes I could, and I did."

" When did you learn that?" said he, with surprise.

" Since I have been 'bird tenting.' "

" Indeed!" said he, laying down his knife and fork.

" Yes, and he asked me if I should like to go to the Grammar School."

" I said I should like it very much. He then asked me my name, and said he was much pleased, and that I should hear from him again."

" And is that all?" said he, with a disappointed look.

"No; he said there were to be three boys admitted into the school free of cost, and there is to be an examination. That is, those boys who answer the most questions the best are to be admitted."

"Yes, my son, you have my free consent to try, and I hope you will succeed; but I have many doubts about it, as there will be many try to obtain admission."

"George Lightley is going to try, and his father is to hire a private tutor to prepare him for the examination, and he says that none are to be admitted but gentlemen's sons."

"O Frank," said Susan, "I do hope you will get in, and be dressed like those young gentlemen who are there."

"So do I, Sue."

"Don't call me Sue, Susan is my name, if you please."

"If I get there I can help John as well; what I learn in the week, I can come and teach him on Saturdays and holidays."

"My dear Frank," said my mother, "don't talk about it as if you were so sure, for fear of a failure. There will be many candidates, and, of course, many disappointments. If you wish to succeed you must work hard before the time comes, and be prepared for it."

"I will work," said I, as I walked into the field the next morning. "I have heard father say, 'The best way to attract fortune is to be prepared for her coming.' Fortune! why there is no such thing; it is just as people work or otherwise. If I get into the Grammar School by hard and well-timed labour, I shall be fortunate, but if I do not work till it is too late then I shall be unfortunate. People talk about ill fortune, why it is as plain as possible in most cases the result of their own actions. 'I am always unfortunate,' says one, 'I cannot think the reason.' Because you neglect to do things at the proper time, or you do not do them properly. Look at old Farmer Green, he never sows his corn till it is too late, and because he does not get a crop he is unfortunate. I will work now, which is the right time, and if I fail I shall not have to blame myself for it."

CHAPTER XIV.

MR. LIGHTLEY.

TIME rolled on with its unheeded pace, the harvest was gathered in, the potatoes were dug and securely stowed away, the early frosts began to show signs of approaching winter, the leaves began to fall in showers from the trees, the summer birds were departing to warmer regions, and the winter birds began to arrive. The 25th of October was fast approaching, which was to decide my fate.

" Only a week," said I to father one evening, as we were returning from the fields, " to the examination, and I have not heard a word about it. I hope they have not forgotten me."

" I cannot say, Frank," was his only reply.

" But, father, don't you think I ought to know?"

" The trustees know their own business best, and I have no doubt, that if it is their intention that you should be examined, they will let you know. I think if you were to ask Mr. Lightley, he would tell you all about it, as he is one of the trustees."

" But, father, I do not like to go, as George is going to try; and perhaps Mr. Lightley would not like it."

" It is your business, my son; and if you cannot attend to it you are not worthy of the honour which you wish to attain. There is nothing, as I have often told you, that is worth having, but there are difficult and disagreeable duties to perform to attain it. There is only one way to attain to it, and that is to make up your mind and do it."

" But Mr. Lightley is such a cross, ill-tempered man."

" I am aware of it, my son, and that is your difficulty. It is that which hinders you from ascertaining whether you are to go to the examination or not. If you look at it, it is simple enough. Go to the door this evening, and ask if he is at home; and all you have to do is to ask for what you want, and it is done."

My father spoke in such an encouraging tone that what he said appeared quite correct, and the great big difficulty dwindled down to a simple errand on my own account.

What a fuss some people do make about their troubles, which, if they looked them steadily in the face, their great load of difficulties would often dwindle from mountains to molehills. Father often says, it is not half so disagreeable to overcome a difficulty as it is to dread it.

With these and such-like reflections, I arrived at Mr. Lightley's; but with all my resolution I wished it was over. With a profound sigh I raised the knocker, which immediately set a dog barking most furiously in the passage; then a loud angry voice intended to silence the dog; then a howl, which sounded as if the dog had been kicked into order, and the door opened, which set the dog barking again.

" Well, Frank, what do you want?" said Mr. Lightley -for it was he who opened the door.

" If you please, sir," I began, but my voice was lost in the noisy barking of the dog.

" Drat that noisy beast!" said the farmer, catching up a broom, " I will give him such a sore head as he shall not get over in a day or two. I never heard such a din and racket in my life. There that will settle you, I'll warrant, you noisy varmint," at the same time flinging the broom at him. " Now, Frank, what do you want?"

" If you please, sir."

" Dick," shouted the farmer to a man across the yard, " Did you bring that rake out of the field, as I told you?"

" No, sir."

" Why did you not?"

" Because I forgot it. Here is Alfred Day wants you, sir."

" Well Alfred, what do you want?"

" Please, sir, Mr. Grove wants to borrow your spade."

" Where is his own ? "

" Broke."

" Who broke it ? "

" Joe Smith."

" What was he doing with it ? not working I know."

" No, he was digging a weazel out."

" And what right had he to be wasting his time digging weazels, I should like to know ? "

" To catch it, if he could."

" What did he want with the filthy varmint ? "

" To kill it, because it sucked the partridges eggs."

" You can have it, but don't you break it digging weazels."

" No, sir."

" Now, Frank, what do you want ? "

" If you please, sir, I am come to ask you if I may be examined in the Grammar School."

" Eh ! What did you say ? You want to get into the Grammar School."

" I should like to try if you will let me."

" I cannot hinder you as I am aware ; come in the house and I will take your name down. You have come just in time, as I shall not receive any more names after to-night. What is your name, age, father and mother's name, &c., &c. ? " said he, writing it down in a book. " Take this paper and get Doctor Brown to sign it, and you can be at the examination. I think it is very foolish for you to try."

" I hope not, sir, for I have worked very hard."

" I dare say ; but what is the use of your working ? What have you done to what George has ? I even fear for him, as there are thirty-six candidates for the three scholarships ; the greater part of which have been to excellent schools, and what can you do against such as these ? "

" I can but try, sir."

" To be sure, we are always wanting what we are not likely to get, that is human nature. I would not give a straw for your chance."

"There is no harm in any one trying to do their best," said I.

"O no, not the slightest; but there are some people who would set the world on fire to gain their ends; just as you please, good night."

"Father is right after all about doing things at the proper time," said I, as I walked quickly home. "If I had gone a week sooner it would have been better. Nothing like doing a thing at the proper time, as old Mr. Clinker the blacksmith used to say to his son, Sam, when he pulled a hot iron out of the fire, ' Now is the time, Sam,' the old man used to say, ' strike when it is hot, one blow now is better than two the next minute.' I have often found the old gentleman's words true as I have gone through life. Many a good opportunity is lost, by not attending to it at the proper time. Father used to say, ' Do it now, it may rain to-morrow; you may be ill, or something may turn up to call you another way, and thus your business will be neglected till it is too late.' "

With what pride did I lay the papers on the table when I entered the house. I would not have exchanged places with any boy I knew. I felt I had achieved something, and who is there among us who, when we have accomplished a great or good action, does not feel the same.

"There, father, you are to sign this paper, Doctor Brown is to sign that, and I must sign this," said I, with great dignity. How big I thought myself as I talked about signing papers, and then I walked backward and forward across the kitchen the same as I had seen father do when he was thinking.

———

CHAPTER XV.

THE EXAMINATION.

MONDAY, October the 24th, came at last. It was a beautiful fine autumn morning, with a light mist which the sun was gradually melting away, and there was every appearance of a fine autumn day.

All night I could not sleep for thinking about the examination; wondering what sort of a place the Grammar School was inside, and how I should like it. Then I fell into a doze, and dreamed that I could not answer one question, and that George Lightley was making faces at me, and calling me a little beggar. Then there was the head master, in a cap and gown of such wondrous construction that it appeared nothing short of a miracle how he got out of them. Then I saw lots of long serious faces were all staring at me with great eyes; and when I tried to get out of the way I could not move. In this uncomfortable manner I passed the greater part of the night, and as rest was out of the question, I arose as soon as the least dawn of day appeared, and began to look my books over. I could not attend to them, and besides, Doctor Brown says that I ought not to look at a book for a week before the examination. Then I went and cleaned my Sunday boots, and brushed my best suit of clothes. "There," said I, as I set down my boots, which were patched and mended by my father in two or three places, "that is putting a shine on them," and at the same time looking at them most admiringly. Then, how I washed my hands and face; but do all I could, the soap and water would not wash my sun-browned labour-marked hands white.

The clock struck nine, and by a quarter past I was ready. Susan tied my necktie on with a peculiar tie which she had seen worn by a boy at the Grammar School; mother brushed my hair, and put my cap on, and told me "to be sure and stroke my hair down with my hand when I took my cap off." John said, "he would fling the old shoe after me for luck." "There, mother, don't he look nice," said Susan, "just like one of the Grammar School boys. I am sure he will get in, he looks so much like one of them. If he don't, he ought, so hard as he has worked. I am sure George Lightley has not worked half so hard as he has."

"Frank will do his best, I am sure," said my mother,

" and we must leave the result to follow. Now here is your penknife and ruler." " Don't forget the blotting-paper," said Susan. " You will remember what father told you last night about your spelling; if you cannot spell a word correctly when you are writing, use another. And, Frank, don't forget to cross your *t's* and dot your *i's*, as it makes your writing look careful; and another thing, I have heard Mr. Pepper say a *t* without a cross is an *l*." " Have you got all you want?" " Good-bye, Frank," said my mother, kissing me tenderly, " and God bless you. Do the best you can. Now, John, he is going; fling the old shoe for luck."

" There! I am sure he will succeed."

With a beating heart I proceeded up the village street, to the Grammar School. On my way, many well-known faces wished me good luck. When I was passing the National School, John Day saw me; he told the others, and out they all rushed, Mr. Pepper at the head, and gave me a huzza, and wished me all sorts of good fortune. It was pretty clear that if good wishes would get me through, I should succeed easily enough.

At a quarter before ten, I arrived, in a most unenviable state, at the Grammar School. The door stood open, and as all was still, I went in, and seated myself on the end of the seat, just inside the door. A few minutes after, the Rector of the parish, and Doctor Long, the head-master, walked into the school; then came some more gentlemen, who shook hands with the Rector and the Master; then they began to talk very loudly, and look at their watches; then came a carriage, out of which stepped some boys and a lady; then came Mr. Lightley and George. How beautifully George was dressed, and how handsome he looked; and his tutor was with him, who kept whispering to him every minute. I wished I was like George; but what is the use of wishing?

Here my thoughts were cut short by one of the gentlemen calling " silence," at which I started as if a thunderbolt had been thrown at my feet. " Now, young gentlemen, answer to your names, and take your places as you are called over."

To think of me being called a young gentleman,—it was the first time in my life. The names were called over one after another, till at last came—"Frank West."

When all were seated, about a yard apart, and everything was in readiness to begin, Doctor Long said he should like to say a few words to us before we commenced. We all stood up. He then told us what an important undertaking it was in which we were about to engage. It was an epoch in our lives which, to those who were successful, would be the first step to an honourable position in life, if they conducted themselves with that propriety which was necessary to the well-being of the school. One thing I beseech of you, and that is, do not attempt to copy from each other, for in so doing you are deceiving yourselves, and guilty of deception, which will be punished by expulsion from the examination. The subjects in which you are to be examined will be in writing. You will each receive a printed paper of questions, which you are to answer as well as you can. The subjects for examination are Scripture and Religious Knowledge, Arithmetic, including Fractions and Decimals, The First Book of Euclid, and Latin Grammar.

When he had finished speaking, a murmur of talking began, and might be heard, " I have done no Euclid"— " I have done no Latin"—and a third, "It is not fair." " Silence, gentlemen," was again called; the pens and paper were distributed, and then came the first paper, which was on Scripture.

What a time the man did seem in distributing them, and how eagerly each one clutched his paper; and then, with what devouring eyes they were scanned over.

" Yes," said I inwardly, as I looked over the paper, " I can do the first question, and the second also,—the third, fourth, fifth and—yes, the last."

I soon forgot everything around me, and proceeded cheerfully and in good spirits with my work.

A public examination is an exciting affair, even to persons who have no real interest in it. I have since seen many examinations, and have often watched the various emotions that are produced when the paper of questions is being given out. One person takes it with all the indifference imaginable, looks over it, pulls the paper towards him, dips a pen in the ink, and begins at once. Another reads the paper from beginning to end, lays it down, takes up a pen, feels its nib, mends it, shuts his knife slowly and accurately, pockets it, and deliberately commences writing. Another reads the first question, flushes crimson, and a moment after is as pale as death. Others look over their papers, then lay them down, and by their looks they seem to say—"just what I expected"—and look as if they would like to gossip over them for half an hour. In ten minutes from the commencement not a sound is heard, but the scratching of pens, the fall of a ruler perhaps, or the hard ticking of a clock. Occasionally may be seen a person staring with great stony eyes at a tree, or a brick wall, out of the window. You feel inclined to look in the same direction, wondering what he can be gazing at with such earnestness. You can see nothing particular; no more does he. He is thinking; trying to call up some fact which ought to be in his memory. His countenance changes to a light smile; he has got the idea, and in a few seconds his thoughts are down on the paper. This troublesome thought perhaps is the first link to a whole chain of ideas.

Another person sits and cuts a pen, and you would think that he is idling away his time in a very foolish manner, but it is not so; he is thinking. About an hour after the commencement of the examination, the first one rises with a pale face, and leaves the room—he can do no more; as soon as the door is closed after him all remains silent again for a few minutes, and another rises and leaves the room. Some seem neither to see nor hear anything, but keep on steadily writing till within a few minutes of the allotted time, when they lay down their pen, blot the writing, and then proceed to read it carefully over, occasionally putting a cross here, a dot there, underlining some forcible expression, or scratching out a small blot; then the india rubber is applied, so that the paper may appear to the eyes of the examiners as fair and neat as possible. When all is done that can be done, they leave their papers where they have been sitting, and quit the room. If the person has read well for the examination, before he has got twenty yards from the building, he remembers some important part of the subject which ought to have been mentioned, and which he has entirely forgotten. This puts him in fear that he shall not succeed. He meets an old friend, who asks him how he has got on.

" Pretty well," is the usual reply.

" What answer did you give to such a question ?"

" I answered in such a manner," is the reply.

" Then you are wrong, depend upon it."

" Who is your authority ?"

" Beany says so-and-so ; you are wrong. It was a booby trap you may depend upon it."

This sets his mind in a ferment again ; he rushes to his books, and finds that after all he is right and his friend wrong.

While talking about a public examination I had nearly forgotten myself.

" There," said I, as I laid down the pen, " I have answered every question. Now I will just look over it, and dot the *i*'s and cross the *t*'s as Susan says ; take out that ugly blot, and—"

" Now, sir, time's up ; you must give in your papers," said a loud voice.

I looked up for the first time since I began, and I found that I was the only boy in the room, and it was one o'clock.

" Cannot wait, sir—must bring it up immediately, or I shall refuse it."

The papers were given up, and as I carried them to the gentleman, how I admired the beautiful round-hand in which they were written ; and wished father, mother, and Susan could see them.

When I left the room, a knot of boys stood outside, among whom was George Lightley; the others I did not know; but as soon as I appeared, I heard one of them say, " Let us have a bit of fun with him;" accordingly one of them stepped in the path before me, and began with,—

" Well my precious, and what have you done !"

" Pretty well, thank you, sir," I replied.

" O certainly," was the reply. " How is your father and mother, and all at home ?"

" Do you know my father and mother, sir ?" said I, with great simplicity.

" Know them ? of course I do; I have known them for years, and jolly old chaps they are too." At this they all set up a loud laugh. " Now don't be offended, young man, but do tell me who made your boots, because I like the style of them so well, that I really must have a pair just like them ?"

" Don't teaze the little fellow, Rogers," said a tall good-looking boy with curly hair, whose name was Andrew Harker.

" I shall do as I please with him for all you, Mr. Harker. Come here," said he, grasping me tightly by the arm, and opening his knife with his teeth, " I should like to have a lock of your hair, it really is so beautiful—and I must too."

" Give over, Rogers, and let him go, or it will be worse for you," said Harker, stepping forward in a most determined manner.

It appeared that he knew Harker too well to require twice bidding, for he let go my arm, and I made my escape.

When I had got out of their clutches I ran home, and in my excess of joy, I insisted upon kissing them all round; then I told them all about the examination, and that I was sure to succeed, for I had done more than anyone else. I was to go again in the afternoon and evening, and then it would be over, and how nice it will be to hear that I am successful.

All this time there was something looming in the

distance, which often caused me to be silent. There was the Latin Grammar to come, of which I knew nothing, and, consequently, could not take the paper.

In the afternoon we were all seated again in the same place, and the questions were the much dreaded Latin Grammar, with a few questions in English Grammar. In vain, I read the Latin, but it was no use, as I could not do one question. The English Grammar was easy enough, and I did the three questions, which was all the paper contained. I sat for a short time, and then with a sorrowful heart took my cap and left the room.

"It is done," said I, sobbing. "I may make up my mind to a life of toil; I shall fail now, as I had heard one of the boys say, all who could not do the Latin would not be admitted."

"West," said a voice behind me, "the next paper is at six o'clock." On turning round to see who was the speaker, I found it was Doctor Long, the Head Master. "I am sorry to see you look so disappointed, my young friend, I suppose you know nothing about Latin?"

"No, sir; I never had a chance of learning it."

"Then it is no disgrace not to be able to do the questions, but you may be more successful this evening, which I hope will compensate for your not being able to do the paper this afternoon. So hope for the best."

It is hard to hope when there is not a shadow left. The picture was fast changing from what it was in the morning. Then I was bright, buoyant, and full of spirits; I saw down a long prospective; there was a comfortable home, a good education, after that a trade, or if I was very successful in my studies, a scholarship at one of the Universities, and afterwards a useful man and a happy life. Now, I could only see Farmer Ball's horses and ploughs, and a toilsome and laborious life, cut off from most of those joys and pursuits which alone gave me pleasure.

I walked slowly home, where I told my woful tale, and where I had consolation enough from Susan.

"What a shame," said she. "I wish there was no

such thing as Latin grammar. I don't see the use of it. I know all about it, Frank. This is some of George Lightley's work; he got his father to get the gentlemen to set you Latin, because he knew you could not do it. Don't you think it is, mother?"

"I cannot say, as I do not understand it; but I dare say it is something very useful, or the gentlemen would not learn it. I am sorry to see you so soon cast down, Frank. If you look at it in the right light, I see nothing to cause you to despair. You did your work well in the morning, and I have no doubt you will be perfectly successful to-night. I know you are disappointed, but what is a disappointment if we look at it in the right light? simply this—we build up hopes which we wish to become realities, when we have no just right to conclude that they will; and, because they do not turn out just as we wish, we are hurt, and at the same time it is our own fault for indulging in wishes which we take for realities."

"But, mother, it is too bad, after all the work"— here the little red-spotted pocket handkerchief was applied to my eyes.

"My dear boy, it is a disappointment to you I am well aware; we are all liable to them; but I thought my Frank had a more manly spirit than to be cast down at what cannot be helped."

"Never mind," said I, at last, "if I cannot do Latin, I can do Arithmetic and Euclid, and see if I don't do something to-night. Who can tell: if I do not get into the Grammar School, I shall get a good situation somewhere else, and shall not have to drive the plough after all. What is the use of fretting, I should like to know?" Here I caught up Moses, and danced round the room, much to his delight, till I was out of breath; then I seized a spade and went to work in the garden most vigorously. "Nothing like work," as father says, "to scare away troubles." After labouring for two good hours, and bringing myself into a calm frame of mind, I sauntered into the fields at the back of our house, down to the mill through the wood, released a poor sheep that was caught in a thorn, and then returned home.

At six o'clock I returned to my work, calm and collected, and in two hours I had done every question, Fractions, Decimals, Euclid, and shown the reason for every step in the working.

"That will do," said I, as I carried up my paper, and home I skipped as light and gay as a bird.

The next morning it was to be known who were the successful candidates, and we were all ordered to be at the school at one o'clock.

What a time it seemed to have to wait; but half-past twelve the next day saw me on my way to the Grammar School, accompanied by all the boys from the National School, who were going to give three mighty cheers if I had succeeded.

As soon as the clock struck one, Doctor Long came into the school with a paper in his hand, and in a moment all was silent as the grave. How my heart beat, and if I had not sat down I think I must have fallen. It seemed as if all the work of my life was about to be destroyed, and by the pale and anxious faces around me my companions seemed to feel the same.

"Gentlemen," began the Doctor, "I do not wish to keep you in suspense, but I wish you to bear in mind that thirty-three will be disappointed. I will now read the list of successful candidates, the first of whom is Andrew Harker—he is good in all subjects. The next is Henry Hemsley." I turned faint. I felt sure it was all over with me. "And the next"—the Doctor paused a moment; every heart beat, for every one hoped it was him—" is Frank West, good in all subjects, and I have no hesitation in saying that if he had taken the Latin Grammar he would have stood first on the list. Gentlemen, you are dismissed."

Here such a shout was raised outside as had not been heard for many a day, and shouts were not unfrequent in that neighbourhood. As soon as I made my appearance, another shout was given that might have been heard a mile.

Alfred Day and John Brand had got an old chair, into which I was thrust, and they carried me in the same manner as if I had been a Guy Faux. Tom Day and Tom Slack had got their mothers' clothes props, and had tied their pocket handkerchiefs together to make a flag. The people ran out to see what was the matter, and when they were told it was little Frank West had got into the Grammar School, they all huzzaed and said, " God bless the boy!" All the while I was so pleased that I did not know whether I was laughing or crying. The Rector shook hands with me, Mr. Pepper shook hands with me, and with the tears running down his cheeks, declared that I was the best boy he had ever had in his school. Some of the women would kiss me; old Farmer Ball shook his stick at me, and finally gave me half-a-crown. In this triumphant manner I was carried from one end of the village to the other, and then home. Mother was so pleased that she declared that she would give all the boys an apple each, to the last one she had, and she did, and had not enough by one, and little Sammy Cliff would have gone without, had not Susan run into the orchard and found one. When the apples were eaten, we huzzaed mother.

CHAPTER XVI.

WHAT THE BAND OF HOPE DID.

Two years have passed away since the events of the last chapter, and during that time I had been carefully and diligently pursuing my studies at the Grammar School. During that period all my spare time had been devoted to the instruction of my brother John, so that with his own striving, he nearly kept pace with me. Susan was still at home assisting mother, as she had a great deal to do, for we had now three cows. Alfred Day was apprenticed to a carpenter, and Alice Slack was gone to a neighbouring boarding school, to be finished off as it is usually termed. Mr. Pepper still continued the mastership of the National School, and owing to my success, he had more than doubled the numbers of his scholars. George Lightley was at home, he had not been sent to any school since his failure at the Grammar School.

During the last two years, the Band of Hope had been slowly, but surely, increasing; the Rector had taken up the subject warmly, and it now began to assume something of an important aspect.

The idea of abstaining from intoxicating drinks at first was a novelty in our village, in which the greater part of the inhabitants disbelieved; but when they found Doctor Brown believed in it, and strongly recommended it to all who came within his reach, people began to think there really must be "something in it."

"It is all very well," said some, "for Frank West to try to do without his beer, but it cannot be done. When harvest comes, that will try if it is what he would have us believe." Harvest came, and my father entered upon his work, and to outward appearance went through his daily labour quite as easily as those who drank two quarts of beer. The great question then arose, did he do as much work, and as well. There could not be the least fault found in that respect. After the harvest was finished, Farmer Ball was heard to say that he thought Frank West a foolish man, but he wished he had half a dozen such men; and as he had drank no beer through the harvest, he intended to give him an extra sovereign when he paid his harvest wages. A sovereign in some persons hands is not much, but in the hands of a working man it is a great deal of money; and an extra sovereign often supplies many a want that could not have been obtained but for its timely aid. William Hutton says, that "a shilling is a large sum of money to a man who can only raise sixpence."

When the neighbours saw that my father kept on regularly and firmly in the cause, made no noisy demonstration about his principles, but saw with their own eyes that he was rising in the world, and that he was now master of three cows; then they came to the conclusion, that after all there must be some truth in it, and, at the end of two years, nearly fifty persons in the village had joined the cause.

I have often heard my father say he did not believe that any man ever was led to become a drunkard through the love of the drink, but the love of the company which usually met at the ale-houses. If a man gives up drink, there is a want to be supplied, and that is, "Where shall he go? and how spend his leisure hours?" There is no place but the ale-house. One person says "Let him keep at home." A labouring man always at home of an evening grows as intelligent about affairs in general as a retired country gentleman would be without his newspaper. The village is his world, and he wishes to know what is doing in it, and to hear that, the public-house is the place where he must go. If his desire for information extends beyond his immediate village, where can he obtain this information? He must go to the ale-house, because there he can hear the newspaper read free of cost. Some may say this is nonsense, why does he not take a paper? Perhaps, for several reasons,—one is, he cannot afford it, and if he could, he could not read it so as to be able to understand it.

My father saw this very clearly, and whilst this state of things continued, it would be in vain to hope for much good, and he determined to take steps to remedy it if possible.

One evening, after his return from work, he put on his best coat and hat, and went to the Rectory, and stated his views to the Rector, who at once saw the great advantages of such a plan; "but," said the Rector, "how is such a plan to be put into practice?"

"My plan is this," said my father, "that we hire a house, and set up an opposition to the *Blue Lion*."

"True; and then the money, Mr. West—the money: where is that to come from to start with?"

"I have been making enquiries, and find that I can

get a good room in the village for one shilling and sixpence per week, ready furnished; and another sixpence per week would find a fire. Thus for two shillings a week a comfortable room may be found, capable of accommodating forty persons. I will undertake," said my father, "for one year, to find a room, with coals and lights throughout the year, for two shillings and sixpence a week."

" But what is your object for meeting together ?"

" For people who choose to pay two-pence, or whatever the charge may be, to assemble together, smoke their pipes, make bargains, talk, sing, dance, read the newspaper, or any books which they choose : in fact, do the same as they do at the ale-houses, with the exception that no intoxicating drinks are to be used, and no swearing or gambling is to be practised."

" The plan you purpose, West, is good, and it shall not be my fault if it does not have a fair trial."

In three weeks from the above interview, a comfortable room was hired, a good fire was kept up every evening, and, in one week, no less than forty-one persons joined what we shall now call the Reading-room, although it had not much pretension to it, as no signs of reading appeared for the first week or two. The Rector occasionally sent a newspaper down, but as often as it came, the old lady who had charge of the room, kindled a fire with it, so that in a literary point of view it was useless.

Reading, like everything else, is an art which requires a great amount of practice. To be able to read well, is not to be acquired without years of constant reading, and often not even then. I do not say that a person cannot learn to read, and even understand what they read, in a short time; but to read so as to be heard with pleasure, is an art which few can arrive at.

One evening, about a month after the opening of the Reading-room, and the novelty of it was passing away, Mr. Pepper purposed to read every evening for an hour, anything that might be deemed useful or entertaining. Of all the readers which it has been my lot to hear, and I have heard many in my time, I never heard one to surpass Mr. Pepper. Everything he read you could remember, and whatever the subject, you wished to know more about it. This was well received by nearly all, and on some evenings the room was crowded. Whatever book Mr. Pepper selected for reading, he always had an eye to the practical utility of it, so that what they heard they understood, and could think about, and as one man said, "turn it over a few times in their minds." Simple tales of Animals, Domestic Economy, Hints to Farmers, and many other works of interest, were read and explained. Often arose a friendly discussion upon a point of farming. The book perhaps recommending, that in fattening a bullock certain kinds of food ought to be used. "Now, I don't agree to that," says one. "Why not?" Then out would come twenty reasons from as many persons that the book was wrong, or that it was right. In this way a vast deal of useful and practical experience was brought forth, opinions were freely given, and as duly weighed and examined, so that none could hear and not learn something. True, the discussions sometimes took a rather warm appearance, but what of that? it showed the parties were interested in the affair, and as there were no strong drinks to urge them on, the disputes always ended in a friendly manner. Some one has said a little knowledge is a dangerous thing : undoubtedly it is, but none at all is much more dangerous. In my experience, when a person has obtained a little knowledge, that knowledge is like a little plant, —only give it a fair chance and it will soon increase. The mind is like all the other great works of the Creator,—once put into action, without some force to hold it at rest, it continually progresses.

Thus it was with our Reading-room. A little knowledge was gained, and with it a desire for more ; and where could that desire be gratified but in reading, and, when once a man takes to reading, the wisdom and experience of ages is within his reach.

In time the reading began to be wearisome, and Mr.

Pepper, urged on by the Rector, offered a prize of a guinea for the best written essay on feeding cattle. This set the young men to thinking and reading, thus, as my father observed, it answered four ends. It caused them to read, to think, to express their thoughts on paper, and led them into habits of study. Nothing so forcibly impresses a subject on a person's mind as writing about it; thus, the subject which was to be brought forth, together with the new plans which they examined, caused them soon to see that the old-fashioned notions that they had adhered to so long were of the most objectionable kinds that could be devised. In course of time new plans were adopted, new buildings were erected, and, in fact, a great transition took place in the village.

Another scheme which was purposed by Mr. Pepper, and carried out with good effect was, to gather a history of the village and the surrounding neighbourhood. This Mr. Pepper undertook to do.

Now, what can be of more interest to anyone than a history of those subjects which he daily sees around him. Here is the church, the bells, the tombs, the churchyard, the village feast, the parish stocks, the village green, and a hundred other things, all of which have histories; and are always interesting to every class of persons. This subject lasted a long time, and was full of instruction and amusement. After the reading of each paper, anyone was allowed to ask a question, in this manner arose much friendly discussion, which brought out ideas and thoughts that were of little use to their owners, but eagerly caught at by others.

Among other things, a great desire for reading became manifest, and to supply this desire, a library began to be talked about, and when once talked about, it was not long before a move was made in the right direction to obtain one. The question was, how was the money to be obtained? This is often a difficult question to answer, but in the present case, no difficulty was experienced. We wanted the library, and that was a sufficient motive for us to proceed at once to get it.

The Rector, as soon as the subscription list was tendered to him, gave five pounds, and it was surprising what a number of signatures there were as a Reader, a Friend, a Guest, with a sovereign attached to each of them.

My father who collected the money would never say who these signatures were, but we knew that they were many of them working men, who, by abstaining from strong drinks, had it in their power to give.

The next thing was a book-case. A man who was a carpenter, offered to do all the wood-work, if anyone else would find the wood. The Rector had a lot of deal boards, which he offered, and the glazier said if they had glass doors for the book-case, he would find glass, and put it in the doors. Another person said he would French polish it, so that no one should know it from mahogany.

Thus a book-case was obtained, with about forty pounds towards furnishing it; in doing which, great care was observed. The Rector said that he thought it would be desirable to purchase a few books at a time, and then see what kind or class the members preferred. If anyone saw a book that they thought would be useful to them it was written down, and at the first opportunity the book was purchased. In this way in the course of time, we had a library of well-selected books, and as the numbers increased, the funds also increased, and new books were constantly being added to the library. If it was perceived that a book was not read, and it stood useless on the shelves, it was sold as secondhand, and a new one put in its place.

The next step was the formation of a small cabinet of curiosities. This at first sight may seem a simple thing; but it is surprising the interest working-men take in a small museum collected by themselves. In our neighbourhood had been fought two famous battles, so that in digging it was no uncommon thing to find old rusty pieces of armour, an old spur, a coin, a glaive, a gauntlet, which, when collected together and cleaned, soon began to form a case of curiosities that to the collectors were valuable.

The younger members, such as Alfred Day, my brother John, Susan, and Alice Slack, purposed to furnish a cabinet of snail-shells, of which no two were to be of the same species. When this was accomplished came the fossils, which in our neighbourhood were rather scarce; but even these were occasionally found and added to the general collection. Then there arose a cabinet of miscellaneous articles, such as a remarkable bird's-nest, a hornet's-nest, an iron ring, a tooth of some monster that had been found in the gravel-pits, and such articles as were occasionally found in the neighbourhood. The next case was of stuffed birds, such only as could be found in the immediate locality, with one of their eggs if it could be obtained. In this manner, in a remarkably short time, a collection of things were got together, showing the history, geology, natural history, and the productions of the village, nearly all of which were collected by the working-men.

Some may object to this, on the ground that it hindered them in their work. I can only say they never went out of their path for any of the various curiosities they were daily bringing to the Museum; but simply if anything came in their way, they picked it up and carried it to the Rector, who pronounced if it was of any worth; if not, the finder might do as he pleased with it.

A few words upon the effects of the Band of Hope. In the expressive language of old Tom Callatt, the landlord of the *Blue Lion*, when asked his opinion of things in general, " Why," said he, " I may pack up my traps, and so may old Joe Hicks, the constable, for what he can get to do in that line; for to my certain knowledge he told me, almost with tears, that there had not been the shadow of a row for nearly two years." " I believe you, Joe," said Tom, giving his head a mournful shake, and puffing from his mouth huge volumes of tobacco smoke. " Now, Joe, you will hardly believe me when I tell you, that twelve months ago I brewed six butts of the strongest treble X, and there it stands, and there it is likely to stand, unless I drink it myself. Things are come to a strange pass when a man cannot live by his labour. I have known the time, Joe, when that quantity of ale would have been gone in a week. Those were the times when I have had to send for you twice in a night."

" You are right, Tom."

" As for a row, now, people have not got spirit enough in them to get up one."

" I think so too, Tom, and what things are coming to I cannot see for the life of me. The fact is this,— your trade and mine are about over. Old Doctor Brown was saying that he had nothing to do now, and so the old boy has taken a few acres of land to amuse himself with."

" That serves him right," said Tom; " for he was the first mover in the affair of total abstinence as they call it."

" Now, Tom, is it not a queer fact, that just as your trade and mine go down, up goes the parson's; for last Sunday the church was full, so that there was scarcely a seat to be got. Now, if you will believe me, I went out of curiosity from one end of the village to the other, during service time, and I did not see man, woman, or child, in the streets."

" 'Tis sad, very sad, to think about, Joe. Bless me! I have known the time when this green in front here has been covered with men and boys from six in the morning till dark at night. There used to be all sorts of games going on: I have drawn four barrels of beer on a Sunday on an average through the year. That was the time to live. You see those two-gallon cans hanging there; they have not been used now for above two years, and I am afraid they never will again. If things don't alter in a few months, I shall take the old *Lion* down and give it up; but I think 'twill break my heart, Joe, to do it. To think that he has swung there for nearly sixty years, to my certain knowledge, offering ' good entertaiment to man and beast,' till nobody believes a word about it. If it was not wicked, Joe, I wish I had died when I got run over coming from Welton, and then I should never have seen the

G

like of this.   But it is no use complaining, for as the saying is, what cannot be cured must be endured." Here Tom knocked the ashes out of his pipe, and taking another pull at his treble X, gave the mug to his companion and told him to " drink it up, for his heart was too full to enjoy it."

CHAPTER XVII.

A LITTLE ABOUT GEORGE LIGHTLEY.

" I TELL you what, Mrs. Lightley, it is time George began to do something," said Mr. Lightley one evening as he was sitting by the kitchen fire.

" Is he not doing something every day," retorted Mrs. Lightley sharply; " I cannot think what you would have; you are enough to worry the boy's life out."

Mr. Lightley smoked on in silence for a minute or two, and then slowly said, " Mrs. Lightley, George will never make a farmer."

" No, he is too good for that; he is born to be a gentleman, and a gentleman he shall be if I can rule it.

" It is the duty of every parent to put his children into some trade or profession, so that they may be able to obtain a living in a respectable and honest manner, and as George seems not cut out for a farmer, I am determined to put him to something else.   I should like to know what he prefers to be, and then we must find the means to place him in it."

" I do not see that he can do better at present than as he is," said Mrs. Lightley, who could not bear the thought of George going from home.

" It must be, Mrs. Lightley.   George shall never have to accuse me in after-life of not putting him into a way of getting his own livelihood."   When Mr. Lightley said a thing must be, all knew that it was final, and that there would be no changing his mind.

"Well, my son," said he, when George appeared, "where have you been all day?"

"We have had such fun at the steeple-chase; two of the jockies thrown from their horses, one has hurt his back, and the other the doctor thinks cannot get over it; and Squire Allform's mare has hurt herself so much that they will have to shoot her. I won three half-crowns on the race; it was a good job the Squire's mare got hurt, or I should have lost my money. I am going to-morrow to a pigeon shooting—I have got a bet on young Jack Hills, and if he does the trick right I shall be safe to win a sovereign. Jack is a capital shot, I saw him shoot two ——"

"I think, George, you would be much better at home assisting me in managing the farm than going about among so many loose characters; for although these steeple-chases and gamblings are got up by gentlemen, I cannot help thinking that you would be best away from them."

"I hate farming," said George, "and I do not see the harm, when one has the time, of seeing a little life."

"I have come to the conclusion, George, that such company are no good to you, and also it is my intention to put you to some trade; and I wish to know what it shall be. Any business you think that you should prefer, I shall be glad to find you a situation at."

"I do not want to be a trade—it is so slow, and I should never shine in it," said George.

"We are not born to shine, but to labour; and no business will ever pay any man unless he follows it carefully, honestly, and thoroughly."

"And that is just what I never could do. I could not stand behind a counter all day to wait upon a lot of fellows who do not know what they want, and think that you are cheating them all the time you are doing your best to serve them."

"If you would not like a trade, what do you say to a profession? A parson is not so bad, but then you will not study for it. What do you say to a lawyer ?"

" That I should never make one.   I consider that a remarkable slow business, to sit poring whole days over musty parchments ; and then you know it takes a deal of learning, and that is what I shall never have the patience to acquire."

" What do you say to a doctor ?"

" That is a little better, but they say there is a lot of things to learn before one can make it out. I should like to ride in a gig, and have a fast-trotting nag, and a tiger in buttons and all that ; and another thing, the pay is good.   Yes, a doctor would do very well if it was not so troublesome to learn.   If I had my choice I should prefer the army ; I think that is about the most gentlemanly profession that one can enter into."

" That is what I can never consent to, George, as in the army you would not be happy ; and the duties of an officer in the army are often very unpleasant.   It is all very well to look at, but you do not see beneath the surface : every officer in the army is under the control of those above him, and cannot even leave his regiment without leave.   No, George, anything but that."

" I do not know—I do not care about anything in particular."

" I have heard of a situation to-day which I think will suit you well, and is not far from home."

" I hope it is not anything that has much work about it."

" George, I fear you will find but few situations in which you will have to labour either with your head or your hands, and perhaps with both."

" But the situation, father,—I am impatient to hear what it is."

" What do you say to a cattle-doctor ?"

" Capital !   Why, I am just the lad for it."

" Mr. Dixon, of Welton, is in want of an apprentice, and he has been asking me about you."

" Yes, I should like it much ; he is a capital fellow,

I saw him take one of the finest leaps on that grey mare of his that I ever saw in my life; and what a sight of dogs he keeps, enough to eat him out of house and home."

"I told him that I would hear what you had to say, and if the profession suited you, I should have no objection."

"I think," said Mrs. Lightley, "George would shine in such a situation if he was well dressed, and carried himself in a gentlemanly manner."

"I do not want him to shine as you call it, I want to see him a useful man, and able to earn his living by his profession."

A few days after the agreement was signed and sealed, and George was to go to his new home the following week.

"Now, George," said Mrs. Lightley, "I hope when you leave me, that you will always hold you head up, and not forget the lesson I have taught you about respectability. If you condescend to do any dirty work which Dixon may think proper to set you to, I should at once refuse, as you go to be a doctor, and not a servant."

"There is another thing which makes a gentleman, which you have not said a word about, mother."

"What is that, George?"

"Money! no man can behave like a gentleman unless he has plenty of money."

"In that case, I hope you will spend as little as you possibly can. Remember, you have lost a great deal lately in your foolish bets; I dare not let your father know anything about it; if I did, I am certain he would be very angry."

"But, mother, you will tip me a five-pound note now and then; won't you now? there's a dear old soul," and then George threw his arms round his mother's neck and kissed her. He knew she could never refuse him after that.

"Well, George, I shall see how you behave; if your conduct is such as I approve, perhaps I may."

" Now, George," said Mr. Lightley, " you are going from home for the first time, and I hope you will always remember that one of the first duties of a servant to his master is to study his interest in preference to his own."

" I will see to it, father; I shall get on capitally, I am sure."

" Another thing, my son, and that is, I hope that you will give up the habit of gambling, for it has been the ruin of thousands, and is one of the worst vices that mankind has ever been addicted to. It is one of those vices from which there is no return; once get into the stream, and your whole course is down, down, to the ocean of ruin, from which there is no redemption. It is dangerous for a man to win, and it is equally dangerous for him to lose. If he wins it urges him on to greater lengths, and so absorbs his thoughts from his business that his daily duties soon become irksome to him. If he loses, his thoughts are wholly bent on regaining what he has lost; he is always in a turmoil, he is never happy, and can find no pleasure but in the pursuit of gaming. I have often heard young men say, there is no harm in betting a small sum; but let me tell you, George, that there is as much danger in betting small sums as there is in a man hanging by a rope over a deep pit, and cutting the rope with his own hands. There is much harm in a small bet—it is the first approach to danger; and if you win you are sure to bet again, and if you lose, you are more eager than ever to make up your losses. A gaming man is generally a drinking man; if he wins, he drinks because he imagines he can afford it; if he loses, he drinks to calm his nerves for a more successful venture. Thus drinking and gambling go on together, and when once these vices get possession of a man, he must possess a very strong mind to be able to forsake them. The usual end of all gamblers is the hulks, or even worse than that. I have often heard men say that they mean to go just so far, lose so much, and when that was done stop. It is easy to say so, but not one in ten thousand stop till they get beyond the bounds of honesty, when the law lays hold of them, and they are ruined for life. A gaming man and a drinking man are, in my opinion, the worst characters there are, and it is your father's wish, George, that you may never become either."

"Never fear, father," said George gaily; "I intend to be just what you wish me."

"I hope you may." And with these words they stepped into the conveyance which was to bear him to his new home.

CHAPTER XVIII.

GEORGE LIGHTLEY'S APPRENTICESHIP.

"This is a rare beginning, and no mistake! Two horses to clean, their harness to attend, sweep the yard twice every day, and when there is nothing else to do, hammer away at this iron pestle, which is almost as heavy as a pavier's rammer. From morning to night it is just the same,—the same horses to clean, the same harness to black, the same pestle, and for all this work the same abuse from old Dixon. I cannot think what father could be thinking about to send me to such a master as this!"

Such were the reflections of George Lightley one morning, a few days after he had been an inmate at Doctor Dixon's. And such are the reflections of thousands of other poor inefficient youths who are brought up in the world till nearly manhood before they are taught that labour is the duty of everyone, from the highest to the lowest in the land. How often do we hear parents say, as an excuse for their folly in not compelling their children to perform some duties, "Why he will work when he gets older." And what are children doing till that period comes?—contracting habits of idleness and a lawless freedom, which will be the bane of their lives. If a parent does not find useful employment for his children, the children will find it for themselves, and it is often of that kind which is not the best suited to their morals. It is imprinted in our nature to be in action, and unless those actions are properly directed in childhood, it is a thousand chances if they are not misdirected through life. A man on the eve of transportation once said, when asked what was the first step which led him astray; "A too common one among parents," was his reply: "I was allowed to do as I pleased when a child, which was the germ from which in after-life sprang all my misfortunes." Allowing a child to remain in idleness, or to seek his own amusements, is one of the greatest follies of which a parent can be guilty; not but that amusements are essential to a child, and it is right that they should follow their amusements as often as they can find time; but let every child have his or her duties to perform, and from those duties there must be no appeal, except in sickness. Play, to a child under such circumstances, is a pleasure, but under other circumstances it is often nothing but idleness.

"I wonder what old Dixon is thinking about, not to allow me to go to the races with him to-day. He could have taken me in his gig just as well as not, and as for what I shall do at home, it won't be worth a deal, I will take precious good care. I see no fun in working when everyone else are taking their pleasure, and if I cannot go to the races, I must contrive to pick up a little amusement at home. I wonder whether Jack Marks is at home,—I will run and see." And throwing down his pestle, away he posted to the *Rose and Crown*, and to his inexpressible joy his friend had not gone to the races, much to his own disappointment, and was consequently in no very amiable mood, and to use his own words, "It was a shame to keep a fellow at home, when he had three bets on the handicap."

"Well, my swell, and what's the game, eh?" said the worthy of the *Rose and Crown*.

"How is it you are not gone to the races, Jack?"

" Why, if you wishes to know particularly, you must ask the governor when he comes home, but it is against my own private feelings, that I am not gone."

" I say, Jack, cannot we have a bit of fun of some sort at home ?"

" I am fly for any manner of thing that is in the shape of fun ; but what is it to be ?"

" I don't know : Is old *Pincher* at home ?"

" Yes."

" Cannot we get up a dog-fight ?"

" Why, the fact is this : the old governor has set his head against dog-fighting, and the last time I fought him, I got a most precious licking ; so you see it is not quite the thing. Those lickings are not comfortable. Suppose we get a boat and have a row down the river as far as the *Three Swans*,—have a game at anything you like for a glass, and back again."

" I do not understand boating," said George, " and I should say no." George had a very tender recollection of boating, for the last time he got into a boat he managed to tumble into the river, and was fished up with a boathook, nearly drowned.

" Then what else shall it be ?" said Jack, as you seem so particular this morning.

" Have you got a gun ?"

" Yes ; but the governor has it locked up in a closet. Your master has one, a double-barrel, one of the best in Welton. He gave thirty pounds for it, I heard him say so in our house. If you can get that, we can have some fun with rats down the river."

" I don't like to take it, for fear anything should happen to it, and I do not think he would like it."

" That is just the very reason you ought to take it. He makes you do many things you don't like, so you see it is only giving it home again."

" What time shall you be ready, Jack ?"

" When you please. I will go down now, as I have nothing to do."

" I have six bottles of medicine to mix ; one each for a calf, two horses, and three cows. That will take about an hour, and then I shall be ready."

Away went the two to the cattle-doctor's shop, and George proceeded to mix the medicine, while Jack amused himself in taking down the bottles, and smelling, tasting, and making comments upon things in general.

"I say, George, now isn't it queer that these nasty stuffs should do the good they do to cattle? What has that great bottle in the corner got in it?"

"I don't know, but the governor always tells me whenever he comes into the shop never to touch it."

"That is a good reason that I should know what it is. It looks like water. It has no smell. I wonder how it tastes!"

"Don't taste it, Jack, perhaps it is poison."

"What is in this bottle?"

"Oil for making salve."

"Let us see how they will mix."

"Jack, you will do some mischief if you do, it will go off as loud as a gun."

"Then we will have a good one." Jack poured a quantity of the colourless liquid into the oil; bang went the mixture, crash went the bottles in all directions, and a sheet of fire burst out all over the room.

The two boys, dreadfully frightened, rushed out of the shop, neither of them much the worse, except their clothes, which were spoilt; for wherever the mixture touched, it burnt holes, for the water-like fluid that Jack had poured into the oil was vitriol.

"You have done it now, Jack," said George.

"I don't care; it is nothing to do with me."

"But you will help clear the shop up, and I will throw some more saw-dust down; and, after all, I can think of something to tell the governor it was an accident; or, I took the wrong bottle in a mistake. I will think of something."

"You are a good one, George. I think we had better be off. Where is the gun?"

"I will fetch it."

Locking the door, these two worthies set off to the river, in search of rats or anything which happened to come in their way. The first object which presented itself was a lark. "Now, George, you have the first shot—blaze away, my boy; that is the way to make the feathers fly." But they would not if the bird had not flown away with them.

The next object that came under their notice was a hare, which Jack managed to hit. "This is what I call sport, George. If we can but bag another or two, it will be all right; I know where to sell them; I can make two——"

"Well, my lads, what are you up to?" said a gruff voice behind them. On turning round, there was Squire All-form's keeper.

"Nothing," said Jack.

"What is that you have in your pocket?"

"Nothing but my pocket-handkerchief."

"You have a hare young man, and as this is not your first offence, I shall prosecute. I know you both, and at the same time wish you to get off the Squire's grounds as soon as possible."

"This is all through you, George."

"Why through me? I did not shoot the hare."

"No, but you would bring the gun out; if you had gone down the river I should not have got into this scrape. It is only a week ago I had to beg the Squire's pardon for poaching; I know what I shall get this time."

"What?" said George.

"A month on the treadmill, as he is a magistrate. I wish the gun and you had been somewhere else before you had got me into this mischief. Here take it, and let both barrels off, or there will be more mischief."

Bang, bang, went the two barrels into the hedge, followed by a groan, and a heavy fall.

"What is that? you have shot somebody," said Jack, peeping through the hedge. "I will be hanged if you have not shot your master's old bull. If you have not done it now. I shall get a month, and you will get off cheap at seven years' transportation. I am sure the Squire will make it out wilfully done."

The two guilty lads hastened to their respective homes, and no sooner had George put the gun in its place than he heard the sounds of his master's gig returning from the races.

"All right, George?" said he, as he got out.

"Yes, sir."

"No one called?"

"No, sir."

"Then run up to the Squire's with the six bottles of medicine, and be back as quickly as possible, for I shall want you."

For the first time it struck George that it was not ready. In the confusion he had forgotten it.

"If you please, sir, I forgot the prescriptions, and did not like to meddle with the drugs for fear of mischief."

"That is very careful, George; never mind, I will see to it."

No sooner had Mr. Dixon entered the shop than he perceived a most horrid smell.

"What have you been doing?" said he; here he gave a low whistle. "You have been to this vitriol—and the oil,—the ammonia jar broke—the turpentine gone —three bottles gone from here—two cracked on this shelf." Taking out his keys, and unlocking the desk, he found his papers and books smouldering, and in a few moments they burst into a flame.

Just when things were at this juncture, in walked the gamekeeper. "Is Mr. Dixon at home?" was his inquiry.

"Yes," said George.

Touching his hat: "If you please, sir, your bull is dead."

"Dead!" said the doctor. "What was the matter?"

"I cannot say, sir; but I think he was shot, for I saw two young gentlemen with a double-barrelled gun, and I heard two shots fired, close to the hedge, and when I went about an hour after I found the bull dead."

"Who were they that had the gun?"

"Your young man was one, and Jack Marks was with him, and if I mistake not, they had your new gun with them."

"That is it, is it?" said the doctor. "This must

be seen into; I wonder things are no worse. It is by the merest accident in the world, that the house and premises are not burnt to the ground."

"Now George, I have only one word to say to you, and that is, you leave this house to-night, and if your father chooses to pay for the mischief you have done, I shall be satisfied; but if not, I will prosecute you for the wilful damages you have committed."

George returned home, and to spare him from disgrace, his father paid the money for the mischief, and George was once more at liberty.

CHAPTER XIX.

A NEW EVENT IN MY LIFE.

I HAD arrived at my eighteenth year, and as yet I had fixed upon no profession. An opportunity now occurred, which opened a way for me to enter one of the Universities. This opportunity only occurred once in three years. The funds of our school provided that three of the scholars should be sent to Cambridge or Oxford, to be supported there for that term. I had been in the Grammar School about six years, and under the able tuition of Doctor Long, I had read deeply in Latin and Greek; I was master of two modern languages, and had mastered some of the higher mathematics, so that on the whole, Doctor Long said he had not the slightest fear but I should do well, and be an honour to any profession that I might adopt.

The last evening at the dear old home. Home never seems half so sweet as when we are about to leave it.

We were all together once again, just as we used to be in days of old. My father sat by the fire, laying and relaying the brands with the tongs, as he always did when he was thinking or troubled. John, who was now a fine youth, was reading Homer, and holding some worsted for mother to wind off his hands into a ball.

Susan was gossiping over the garden gate with Alfred Day; and Moses was nearly asleep in his little chair.

" So you leave us to-morrow, Frank?" said my father.

" Yes, father, for a time; but if I could I would much rather stay with you always."

" No, my son; your path lies before you, pursue it as straight as you have done hitherto, and I shall have no fear for you. But remember the world is full of temptations, of which you have no idea. You have as yet only seen your own village, and lived among your own people; but when you get into the great world of Cambridge, you will be among people who feel, talk, and act differently to what you do. You will find some there who, like yourself, are all simplicity and innocence; while others, whose whole lives have been one manhood, so to speak, are acquainted with all the vice and craft that tends to degrade mankind."

" I will do my best when I get there, father, and I hope to be kept from that which is evil."

" My son, rely upon Him who has said, ' Cast thy burden upon the Lord.' It is He alone who can support you under all temptations and difficulties. When you get away from us you will have none but Him to guide and watch over you. All we can do at home is to pray for you that you may be kept in the strait and narrow road which leadeth to life eternal."

Here Susan and Alfred Day came into the house, and the conversation became general.

" I wish," said Susan, " Frank was not going to leave us; how we shall miss him !"

" I wish I was in his place," said John.

" But you never will be," said Alfred Day.

" I do not take any notice of what you say, Alfred; you said Frank would not get into the Grammar School, but he did, and now has got nearly out of it again."

" But you have not got the head for learning that Frank has."

" Perhaps not; but I think I heard of a place to-day that I could get without much trouble, which would suit me much better than following the plough."

"What is it, John?"

"I hear that an Assistant Master is wanted at Welton Bluecoat School. I think I could manage that pretty well."

"Of course you could," said Alfred laughing, "considering that one-quarter of the boys are bigger and older than you are."

"I can but try it for a while."

"Of course you can; but of all businesses or professions, I hope to be saved from that of a school master."

"Every one to their liking, Alfred."

The next morning I was up as soon as it was light. I kindled a fire, put on the kettle, and went out to take a last look at home. There lay the old axe which I had used many a time; I took it up, examined its edge, and gave it one swing, exclaiming, "The last time!" Then there was old Daisy, Primrose, and Betty, the three cows, to bid good-bye to, poor dumb animals that they were. I felt I loved them as if they had been of the family, and in one sense they might be said to be; two of them had been with us from my childhood, and had been tended and cared for almost as much as we had. The last meal at home, a nice and tempting breakfast—but Frank's heart got fuller and fuller as the time drew near for the stage to arrive. Frank could not eat, although persuaded with all the endearing terms a kind mother and father could think of.

The time arrived at last, I could not find a single excuse for remaining a minute longer. There hung the old slate that I had used so often, and with such zeal. I took it down for the last time, and taking the pencil out of its leather case, wrote, "God bless you all, and think of me when you read this." I then hung up the slate, and at that moment Moses gave a loud whistle, to signify that the coach was in sight, I hastily kissed mother and Susan, ran down the garden path, and arrived at the end of the lane just as the coach stopped.

Six hours slow travelling brought me into the old town of Cambridge, with its narrow streets, its quaint old houses, and ancient halls and colleges. What a sensation it produced in my mind, as I surveyed, for the first time, the exterior af the Colleges. I felt I was on sacred ground. I felt it was here that many of the good, the great, the patriotic, had lived and learned. It was in these time-hallowed cloisters that poets, whose names will be handed down to undying fame, walked, conversed and studied. It was here that sages, philosophers and historians had resided, whose works and whose wisdom will last and edify mankind as long as the language is spoken in which their wisdom is inscribed.

I had not been located long in Cambridge before I became acquainted with its curiosities, its walks, and all those matters which are interesting to a stranger. The first places I visited were the libraries belonging to the Colleges, which consist of hundreds of thousands of books in every written language on the face of the globe.

The Museums are well worth a visit, as they are very rich in curiosities, not only of such things as are found in the immediate neighbourhood, but from all parts of the world. Then there is the picture gallery, in which there are many works of great value, and which are highly prized by the University.

The hospital is a fine building, and is open for the reception of patients from any part of Cambridgeshire. It is supported by voluntary contributions, and has proved of great service to many who, but for that, would have sunk into a premature grave.

There is a large piece of ground called Parker's Piece, which is used for the purpose of recreation; and during the cricket season, scores of sets of players may be seen at one time on the Piece.

The river Cam runs through Cambridge, and, owing to the flatness of the country, it is remarkably slow, and often very muddy. It rises at a small village called Ashwell, about eighteen miles south-west of Cambridge; and is navigable only as far as Cambridge. Owing to the sluggishness of its stream, it is well adapted for boating; a fact of which the students at the University take advantage. On a Saturday afternoon, hundreds of them may be seen plying the oar in their little frail-built boats.

The Churches of Cambridge have nothing particular to boast of, either in their style of building or the elegance of the architecture. The principal is Great St. Mary's. St. Sepulchre is a curious old church; in shape it is round, and is said to have been built by the Knights Templars.

In the centre of the market is the Conduit as it is called; it is a large fountain with eight spouts, which provides water for the market and its neighbourhood. It was built by a carrier of Cambridge, about the time of the great plague in London. This man also brought water by means of a canal from Cherryhinton, a distance of three miles, for the express purpose of supplying the southern part of Cambridge with water. When the water arrives at Cambridge, it does not flow through pipes, as in most large towns, but down the gutters on both sides of the street.

I could tell you a great deal more about Cambridge, had I time to do so; but I must now proceed with more important affairs.

When I had been in Cambridge about three months, I received a letter from home, which ran as follows:—

"DEAR FRANK,—I have according to promise taken this opportunity of writing to you, hoping it will find you well as it leaves us.

"I have no news to tell you, but shall leave that to Susan and John, who have both something to say.

"Your dear mother hopes that you are quite comfortable and happy in your new way of life, and wishes to know if there is any little thing she can send to make you more so; and she wishes me to say she hopes you do not forget to say your prayers night and morning, just as regular as you used to do when you were a little boy.

"I do not think I have anything more to say, only

H

keep your eye on the bright star; don't swerve either to the right hand or to the left. The way is narrow, but plain, and with your Bible and conscience for your guide, and a firm reliance on Him who died for you, I trust you will be able to pursue the heavenward road.

"We remain, dear Frank,
"Your affectionate father and mother,
"FRANK and SUSAN WEST."

Here is Susan's, and this is John's; Susan's first. Now I wonder what she has got to say.

"DEAR FRANK,—I want to see you. When do your holidays begin. Are you quite well. Alfred Day says he hopes you will come and see us at Christmas. Father has bought a new cow; we have four, and the Squire let us have the twenty-acre field, on Rumbal's Road. We are getting on quite well. Old Tom Callat has shut up his public-house. He took the sign down yesterday. Doctor Brown says he thinks the old man won't live long, he does take on so about it. The Band of Hope is very flourishing. There are now two-hundred members belonging to it. They are trying to get up one at Welton, and I hope they will succeed. I do not think I have anything more to say at present, only Alfred Day wishes to be kindly remembered.

"I am, dear brother,
"Your affectionate sister,
"SUSAN WEST."

"That is news," said I, as I folded the letter. "Now for John's."

"DEAR FRANK,—I write to you with great pleasure, as I am happy to inform you that I have got from between Farmer Ball's plough stilts, and am now the Third Master at the Bluecoat School, Welton. My salary is not much for a teacher, but it is much better than it was as a ploughman. I am to have thirty pounds a year with board and lodging, which I think is very good. There is nothing like trying, is there?

" I am doing a little in Theology now. To tell you a little secret, I am looking forward to something higher yet. I have got a good footing on the first step, it shall not be for want of trying, if I do not mount much higher.

" Your old friend Alice Slack is still at Welton. She is Assistant in the school, and I have no doubt she is a very clever girl. I saw her on Sunday last; she asked me how you were, and how you were getting on with your studies. She is not the least like that thoughtless creature who used to laugh at you, and call you her funny old man.

" Since I have been here I have been striving to get up a Band of Hope, the same as we had at home; but as yet we only number sixteen; but I am in hopes to increase it by perseverance. I think it the duty of all of us to do all we can in the cause, considering what the cause has done for us and ours.

" I must now conclude, with wishing you every success in your studies, and every happiness this world can give you.

" I remain,
" Your affectionate brother,
" JOHN WEST."

As I folded the letters, and placed them in my desk, I could not help breathing a silent prayer that those dear friends at home might be always as happy as now.

John's letter is just like him, always trying to do good. I, too, must work yet, although often the flesh is weak when the spirit is willing. John is right when he says he ought to work for the cause of temperance, as it has done a great deal for us, and what would it not do if it was universal? May I live to see the day when it will be so.

CHAPTER XX.

THE LAST.

THE object of my story has now come nearly to an
end, and to pursue it further would be to carry it beyond
my original intention, and would not answer any useful purpose ; all we shall have now to do will be to see
if there is no moral in what has been said ; but before
we come to that, I have a few more things to mention
which all will be glad to hear.

Nearly ten years have passed away since I left the
University, and during that time many changes have
taken place. Many of those we knew had departed
from the earth, and a young and active race were filling
their places.

It is Christmas Eve, and according to my father's
old custom we are all together at his fireside. Not in
the old house, but in the spacious farm-house that was
once Mr. Lightley's, but now my father's. He has
occupied it four years. Mr. Lightley is dead, and George
in one year spent all his father had saved for him, and
then to hide his poverty enlisted as a common soldier,
and died in India. My father looks no older than he
did when I first remember him. There is the same
kind and placid face, the same look of affection, as of
old. A few grey hairs may be perceived, and that is
the only sign of age. He is now sitting in the chimney
corner nursing Alfred Day, jun., and looks as calm and
happy as a man can wish. My mother, true to habit,
is still plying her knitting pins, and if we may judge of
the article she is knitting it is not for any of her children. She looks much the same, with the exception of
her hair, which is as white as silver.

I am now the Rector of our village, and a lady, who
is at this moment trying to set our first-born, Frank
West, and Alfred Day, jun., to dance to her music from
a piano, is my wife—the once giddy Alice Slack. It

seems a difficult matter, and they do not seem to appreciate her attentions.

My brother has now attained the height of his wishes, he is the Head-Master of the Grammar School. Doctor Long is now a Bishop in one of the colonies.

Alfred Day, thanks to the cause, is now in business on his own account, and has, within the last month, entered into a large contract with the railway company, to erect some goods' sheds, which he hopes will be a good speculation. When he was asked where the capital was to come from for him to carry on the work, he answered, "Thanks to temperance, I have plenty of credit."

The *Blue Lion* has disappeared, and on the very site where it stood now stands an elegant building, known by the name of the Temperance Hall.

Doctor Brown is still alive, but very feeble; there is no other doctor in the village, and, thank God, no other is needed.

Mr. Pepper still teaches the National School, and, thanks to the abstinence cause, as he often says, he is in a position to retire any day, only he cannot imagine where another man could be found to whom he should like to commit his charge. There is only one person in the world that he thinks is anything fit for the office, and that is Moses West.

In coming to a close, I wish to ask my young friends into whose hands this book may fall, what you have done for the cause of Temperance? "I cannot do anything," I hear you say; "I should like to be as Frank West or Susan, but I am sure I never shall." You do not know, young friend, what you can do, till like Frank West you have tried,—tried and struggled as they did, and, take my word, if you do not do all the good they did, you can do a little. "I do not see how I can," I hear you say. Well, I will tell you how to do it. Do you abstain from strong drink? "Yes," I hear you say. Have you not some little friend, some little cousin, or some little companion whom you could persuade to do the same? You can do that, and in so doing, you cannot tell the good you are doing,—you may save that young friend from a drunkard's grave. All drunkards were once little children, and as innocent and gay as you. Should you like to see your companions become drunkards? No; you would not. Then ask them to join the cause, and try to persuade some one else.

If every little boy and girl, now under ten years of age, were to join the Band of Hope, where would drunkenness be in twenty or thirty years? Where would be all the manifold institutions which have been erected to suppress drunkenness? The answer would be, " Where are they? " Empty, tenantless, and a home for the owls and bats; or converted into palaces for the refinement and elevation of the people.

I must now bid you adieu for the present, hoping that " The Struggles of a Village Lad" may be read by all the young people of this country, and not only read but practised.

I could still linger on, as loth to leave a work in which I have been as much interested as my young readers; but my sincere prayer at this moment is, may we meet again; if not in this world, in that

" Happy land, far far away."

THE END.

RICHARD BARRETT, PRINTER, MARK LANE, LONDON.

W. TWEEDIE'S

TEMPERANCE PUBLICATIONS.

ALCOHOLICS.—A letter to Practitioners of Medicine, by one of themselves, to show that Intoxicating Drinks should not be prescribed as Medicine. Price 1d.

AUTOBIOGRAPHY OF A BEGGAR BOY; in which will be found related the numerous Trials, Hard Struggles, and Vicissitudes of a strangely-chequered Life; with Glimpses of Social and Political History over a period of Fifty Years. Cloth, 3s.

AUTOBIOGRAPHY OF JOHN B. GOUGH, handsomely bound in cloth, with Steel-plate portrait, 1s. 6d.

A CLERGYMAN'S REASONS FOR TEETOTALISM, by the Rev. W. W. Robinson, A.M., Incumbent of Christ Church, Chelsea, 1d.

A TRACT FOR EVERY CHRISTIAN. 5th Edition of 10,000, each. 3s. per 100.

ALCOHOLIC WINES; a Sermon, by the Venerable Archdeacon JEFFREYS of Bombay, with Notes. Price 6d.

AN EARNEST APPEAL to Christian Mothers on behalf of the TEMPERANCE MOVEMENT. Price 1d.

BITTER BEER. Intended especially to expose the cruel sufferings of Drunkard's Wives. Designed by H. Anelay.

BOOK (The) OF TEMPERANCE MELODY, arranged to Popular Airs. By E. P. Hood. A NEW EDITION, Enlarged, Price 1s.

BREWERS *versus* TEETOTALERS. A Search for Nourishment in a Gallon of Ale; or Plain Facts from the Brewery. On demy folio, for wall or window bills. Price 1d. each.

BRITISH TAXATION; consisting of Five Pyramids, printed in Colours, showing at a glance the Taxation of the Country as compared with the Cost of the Drinking System, with a pointed and practical Statement of Temperance Principles. Price 1d.

BEACON LIGHTS, designed to Warn and to Save. 1d.

BEN CHEERY'S CHRISTMAS BOX, by the Author of "Frank Heath's Manful Strivings." Price 1d.

BOTH SIDES; or, Objection to Teetotalism, by a Medical Practitioner. Price 6d.

CATECHISM FOR BANDS OF HOPE AND YOUNG
MEMBERS OF TEMPERANCE SOCIETIES, in Four Parts. By
John P. Parker. 1d.
- Part 1. Physiological and Explanatory.
- 2. Laws of Health and Chemical Analysis of Food.
- 3. Fermentative Processes and Results.
- 4. Wines of Scripture.

CHADWICK'S (John) M.D., Licentiate of the Royal College of
Surgeons, Edinburgh,) ESSAY ON THE USE OF ALCOHOLIC
LIQUORS IN HEALTH AND DISEASE. Price 2s. 6d. in neat cloth ;
paper 1s. 6d.

CURSE OF GREAT BRITAIN ; showing, by a coloured plate,
the amount of Pauperism, Crime, Disease, &c., caused by Drink, with
Testimonies. 1d.

DEAR BREAD AND WASTED GRAIN. A Lecture,
delivered at the Broadmead Rooms, Bristol, on Thursday, Dec. 20, 1855.
By Thomas Beggs, 2d.

In three parts, price One Penny each.

DIALOGUES FOR RECITATION. By KATE PYER, author of
"Touching Incidents and Tuneful Melodies," &c.
Part I: Dialogue No. 1. "Edward's Danger and his Cure," for two
Youths. Dialogue No. 2. "Anna's Tale. Too Common and too True," for
three little Girls.
Part II. contains a Scenic Dialogue for Three Girls, a Monologue, "Moral
Courage," and several Temperance Songs.
Part III. Dialogue No. 1. "The high Omnipotence of IF !" for two
Youths. Dialogue No. 2, "Rose and Mary." Dialogue No. 3, "Social
Customs."

EXAMINE AND ENQUIRE, by Archdeacon Jeffreys of Bombay.
4 pp., 1s. 6d. per 100.

ESSENCE OF GRAMMAR (The). A Leaf of Love to Save a
Tear. By Henry Mence. 6d.

EVILS OF INTEMPERANCE. A Sermon preached at St.
Clement Danes, on Sunday, Feb. 17, 1856, by Rev. W. Marsh, D.D.,
Hon. Canon of Worcester Cathedral, &c. 1d.

FREEHOLD LAND SOCIETIES ; their History, Present
Position, and Claims. By J. Ewing Ritchie. 2d.

FACTS AND PHASES OF THE TEMPERANCE ENTER-
PRISE. Wrappers 8d., cloth 1s.

A Copyright Steel Engraving,

FROM MAYALL'S LIKENESS OF JOHN B. GOUGH, a
striking Likeness, may now be had. Price 1s.

GOUGH'S AUTOBIOGRAPHY AND ORATIONS, bound in
one handsome volume, gilt edges, with portrait, 5s.

JOHN B. GOUGH'S ORATIONS, singly 1d. each, or 1s. the volume
containing Fourteen.

On Habit.	Are they all Fools who become
Importance of the Temperance Move-	Drunkards?
ment.	The Liquor Traffic.
Address to Children.	Christian Liberty,
The Dangerous Drinking Customs.	Social Responsibility.
	Cause and Effect.

GOUGH'S AUTOBIOGRAPHY, 2d., 6d., 1s. 6d.

GOUGH'S (J. B.) ORATIONS, beautifully bound in cloth, suitable for presents, gilt 2s. 6d.

HISTORY OF BANBURY, before and after a MAINE LIQUOR LAW. By James Cadbury. 1d.

HORRORS OF DRUNKENNESS, illustrated in a Series of Plates taken from the Blessings of Temperance: A Poem by John O'Neill. Sketched by George Cruikshank, Esq. 6d.

HYMNS AND SONGS FOR BANDS OF HOPE. Compiled by the Rev. Newman Hall, LL.B. 1d.

INDIVIDUAL INFLUENCE, by Edward Smith, with an Address to Christian Professors, by Samuel Bowly. Price 2d.

IRRATIONALITY (The) OF DRINKING INTOXICATING DRINKS ; or, the Band of Hope Chairman at his Wits-end. By B. Wood, Minister of the Gospel, Bradford. 1d.

KITTY GRAFTON, a Sad Story of Intemperance, by L. M. Sargeant, 3d.

LIVERPOOL LIFE : its Pleasures, Practices, and Pastimes. By the Author of "Town Life." Reprinted from the *Liverpool Mercury.* Price 1s.

LIVESEY'S TEMPERANCE SHEET, containing 64 Subjects. 1d. each, or 6s. per 100.

"MINE OPINIONS ;" being the substance of an Address delivered to the Members and Friends of the Ebenezer Temperance Society. By the Rev. T. J. Messer. 2d.

MIDNIGHT SCENES AND SOCIAL PHOTOGRAPHS, with a Frontispiece by George Cruikshank. Fancy Boards, 1s. 6d. Cloth, 2s.

MORNING DEW-DROPS. By Mrs. C. L. Balfour. With an introduction by Mrs. H. B. Stowe, written for this work during Mrs. Stowe's visit to this country. 330 pages, price 3s. 6d.

NEW BRUNSWICK LIQUOR LAW (The). Price ½d.

NIGHT SIDE OF LONDON. By J. Ewing Ritchie. Cloth, 3s. 6d. Reprinted from the *Weekly Record.*

NEVER DESPAIR, OR TRUTH STRANGER THAN FICTION. Reprinted from the *Weekly Record.* 129 pages, price 8d.

OBJECTIONS TO THE TEMPERANCE MOVEMENT ; a Lecture delivered in the Corn Exchange, Manchester, under the auspices of the Manchester and Salford Temperance Society. By Rev. Dawson Burns. Price 1d.

O'NEILL'S MORAL POEM, THE BLESSINGS OF TEMPERANCE. Under the patronage of several eminent friends of Temperance, price 1s. stitched. A new and enlarged edition, with illustrations by George Cruikshank ; to which is added a Sketch of the Life of the Author, by the Rev. I. Doxsey.

PLAGUE OF BEGGARS. A Dissuasive from Indiscriminate Almsgiving. By a London Physician. 2d.

PLAIN SENSE FOR PLAIN PEOPLE. By John Sherer, Author of "The Gold Digger of Australia," &c. Price 1d.

POETRY OF CHILDHOOD. By Goodwyn Barmby. Price 1s.

POETRY OF HOME. By Goodwyn Barmby. Price 1s.

PUBLIC-HOUSE TRADE AS IT IS, (The) ; or an Epitome of the Evidence taken before the Committee of the House of Commons on Public-houses. By J. E. Ritchie. Price 3d.

REASONS in Favour of a Maine Law for Great Britain. By W. H. Darby. 1d.

RHYMES AND RECITATIONS FOR THE BANDS OF HOPE. Price 1d.

SCENES IN A GARRET, a Tale of Intemperance. 2d.

SCEPTIC (The) a Domestic Tale. By Mrs. Lee Follen, Authoress of the *Well-spent Hour*, &c. Price 1s., cloth gilt, 2s.

SMALL-POX AND ALCOHOL, Two Poisons ; with Remarks on the Registrar-General's Reports of Deaths occasioned by them. By John Chadwick, M.D. 1d.

SPENCER (REV. THOMAS) PORTRAIT OF THE LATE, 5s., 2s. 6d., and 1s.

TEMPERANCE AND HIGH WAGES ; a Lecture by William Tweedie. Price 1d.

TEMPERANCE IN THE CAMP. A Lecture delivered on the Heights of Sebastopol, Christmas, 1855. By Lieut.-Col. Sir James E. Alexander, Knt., &c., commanding the 14th Regiment. Price 1d.

TEMPERANCE OFFERING ; comprising Essays, Tales, and Poetry, furnished by eminent Temperance Writers. Edited by James Silk Buckingham, Esq. 6d.

TEMPERANCE TALES FOR THE YOUNG. By the Rev. James Ballantyne. Price 6d.; handsomely bound in cloth, 1s.

THE HOUSE THAT JACK BUILT ; with 12 cuts. By G. Cruikshank. Price 1d.

THE GREAT ENEMY ; an Address to Sabbath School Children on the evils connected with the use of Intoxicating Liquors. By a Teacher. Price 1d.

THE SEED AND THE FRUIT. A Temperance Story. Price ½d.

TOTAL ABSTINENCE EXAMINED BY THE LIGHT OF SCIENCE. By John Dyer. Price 6d.

TOUCHING INCIDENTS and Tuneful Melodies. By Kate Pyer. 2d. Second Edition.

TRAFFIC IN INTOXICATING DRINKS (THE) : its Evils and its Remedy : or a MAINE LAW the only hope for ENGLAND. By Samuel Couling. Price 1s.

TRIP TO AYLESBURY AND HARTWELL. By Thomas Irving White. 2d.

TRIUMPH OF TEMPERANCE (THE) ; a Poem, by John O'Neill. Price 1s.

CHRISTIAN TEMPERANCE TRACTS.

www.ingramcontent.com/pod-product-compliance
Lightning Source LLC
La Vergne TN
LVHW061219060426
835508LV00014B/1355